Bouquet of Flowers, from an old American Engraving, 1884.

FOLKLORE and SYMBOLISM of FLOWERS, PLANTS and TREES

WITH OVER 200 RARE AND UNUSUAL FLORAL DESIGNS AND ILLUSTRATIONS

Ernst Lehner
and
Johanna Lehner

DOVER PUBLICATIONS, INC.
Mineola, New York

Bibliographical Note

This Dover edition, first published in 2003, is an unabridged republication of the work originally published in 1960 by Tudor Publishing Company, New York, under the title *Folklore and Symbolism of Flowers, Plants and Trees*.

DOVER *Pictorial Archive* SERIES

This book belongs to the Dover Pictorial Archive Series. You may use the designs and illustrations for graphics and crafts applications, free and without special permission, provided that you include no more than ten in the same publication or project. For permission for additional use, please email the Permissions Department at rights@doverpublications.com or write to Dover Publications, Inc., 31 East 2nd Street, Mineola, New York 11501.

However, resale, licensing, republication, reproduction or distribution of any illustration by any other graphic service, whether it be in a book or in any other design resource, is strictly prohibited.

Library of Congress Cataloging-in-Publication Data

Lehner, Ernst, 1895-
    Folklore and symbolism of flowers, plants, and trees : with over 200 rare and unusual floral designs and illustrations / Ernst Lehner and Johanna Lehner.
        p. cm. — (Dover pictorial archive series)
    Originally published: New York : Tudor Pub. Co., c1960.
    ISBN-13: 978-0-486-42978-6
    ISBN-10: 0-486-42978-4
    1. Plants—Folklore. 2. Plants—Symbolic aspects. 3. Flower language. I. Lehner, Johanna II. Title. III. Series.

GR780.L44 2003
398'.368—dc21

2003055324

Manufactured in the United States by Courier Corporation
42978405
www.doverpublications.com

CONTENTS

STRANGE AND WONDROUS PLANTS

THE FLOWER CALENDAR

THE LANGUAGE OF FLOWERS

Floral Endpiece, by Jean Baptist Michel Papillon, Paris, 1755.

ILLUSTRATIONS

INTRODUCTION

T TOOK *homo sapiens* — the human being — aeons to learn to walk on his two feet, and to turn his grunts into the rudiments of speech, so he could communicate sensibly with his fellow men. It took him thousands of years to discover the making of fire which enabled him to roast and cook his food. It took many more thousands of years to invent the club, the ax, the bow and the arrow, so he could hunt more easily for food animals; to learn how to till the soil, plant and harvest crops; and finally foresake his cave for a dwelling he built himself. And throughout all this time of evolution, where man lived out in the open, he was surrounded by flowers, plants and trees appealing to all his five senses: to his sight, touch, taste, smell, and even to his hearing, warning him by the rustling of leaves and grasses, the rasping of branches, the snapping of breaking twigs, and the crackling of fallen leaves underfoot of any approaching danger by man and beast alike. The behavior of the plants around man was always peaceful and soothing, and man found that there is no such thing as an ugly flower, a menacing plant or an angry tree. Man's mind became attached to these friendly beings, willingly lending themselves to his needs, giving him food and shelter and pleasing impressions for all his senses. Flowers were the first decorative implement for the earliest attempts of man to adorn himself;

they grew all around him and were his just for the taking. Throughout human history flowers, plants and trees became so interwoven with man's daily life that they developed into symbols for his expressions and sentiments, his passions and affections, his beliefs and religions, his fears and superstitions. In Egyptian, Greek, Roman and Nordic mythology, in the Scriptures and Biblical legends, in Oriental beliefs and Occidental lore the fertile human mind assigned the medicinal and nutritious properties of plants, the beauty and fragrance of their leaves, flowers and blossoms as floral symbols to gods and deities, and representations for seasons and months of the year. They became heraldic devices of rulers and states, and badges for heroes and saints; floral emblems of feasts and events, and decorations for religious and worldly ceremonies; flowery expressions of love and desire, and tokens of admiration and reverence. The religious, legendary and symbolic meaning attached to many a plant in bygone days was handed down to us throughout the ages, and is still valid today. We still use many special plants, flowers and trees in accordance with their age-old symbolism for Easter, Christmas, St. Patrick's and other holidays, for weddings and anniversaries, for funerals and memorials, in valentines for mother and sweetheart, and for many other occasions.

The Creation of the Plants, from Coverdale's BIBLIA, *Zurich, 1535.*

SACRED PLANTS

HE FLOWERS, PLANTS and trees surrounding man at the dawn of history changed in a mystical cycle with the seasons. They moved from life to death, and to life again, bearing succulent leaves, sweet-smelling blossoms, juicy fruit, nourishing nuts and life-giving seeds. In the mind of these primitive creatures they became the exponents of some unseen higher spirits who provided mankind with feast and famine. No wonder that man endowed these plants with sacred properties and dedicated providential and supernatural powers to them. The sacred meaning given to some plants in a remote era were handed down from generation to generation, from belief to belief, and from religion to religion. With the changing of time when old idols toppled, and new ones were erected in their place, the dedication of many a revered plant was transferred to the new idol but the sacred character of the plant remained unchanged. Even in our monotheistic Western World of today where the many deities of the polytheistic beliefs have vanished from the minds of men, the sacred plants of old are not regarded as mere objects of utility. They have become the sacred emblems of prophets and saints, and the symbols of religious festivals and holidays.

THE TREES OF LIFE AND KNOWLEDGE

The Trees of Life and Knowledge in the Garden of Eden, from Leeu's BOEK VAN DEN LEVEN ONS
HEEREN, *Antwerp, 1487.*

THE TREE OF LIFE

It is understandable why trees were the first plants to be worshipped by man. They were not only the largest living and growing things around him, but they were also always there; when he was a boy, a youth, a man, an elder. He learned that the trees were already standing in the same groves when his father, and even his grandfather were boys themselves. He saw the trees throughout his lifetime, evergreen or shedding their leaves in autumn, springing to life again in spring, bearing blossoms and fruit season after season, and growing stronger, wider and higher all the time. He grasped the idea that the same trees would still be standing, long after he himself would be gone, when his children would be no more, and his grandchildren would be growing old. No wonder that in man's searching mind, the trees became the very symbols of strength, fecundity and everlasting life. They are Nature's perfect examples of the miracle of reproduction and eternity. It is believed that the conception of the Tree of Life (*Arbor vitae*) started in ancient Chaldea, a region in southwestern Asia along the Euphrates and Tigris rivers. One of the oldest sacred tree symbols is the Assyrian Tree of Life, a stylized,

The Ornamental Tree of Life, from an Ancient Assyrian Wall Carving.

THE TREE OF LIFE

ornamental expression of a non-existing tree, sometimes combining the lotus and the pine, two plants symbolizing immortality and fecundity. These symbols of the Tree of Life spread from ancient Assyria and Babylonia into Arabia, Egypt and Asia Minor, and through Central Asia into the Far East and Central America. Throughout the changing times the tree of life symbols

The Aztec Cosmic Trees Surrounding the Fire-God Xiuhtecutli, from the Old Mexican CODEX FEJERVARY — MAYER, *Liverpool.*

THE TREE OF LIFE

were taken up by all beliefs and religions in the western and eastern world. They range from the oak and ash trees of the Teutons, Norsemen, Celts and Druids to the palm and cedars of the Hebrews and Christians; from the sycamores of the Egyptians to the cassia and bo trees of the Far East, including the cosmic, celestial and humanized trees of many lands.

The Human Tree, by Hans Baldung Grien, from J. Geiler's SERMONES PRESTANTISSIMI DE ARBORE HUMANA, *Strassburg, 1515.*

THE TREE OF KNOWLEDGE

The Fall of Man, by Hans Sebald Beham.

THE TREE OF KNOWLEDGE

In the Biblical Garden of Eden man had to choose between the Tree of Life *(Arbor vitae)*, which was the tree of the immortals, and the Tree of the Knowledge of Good and Evil *(Arbor vel lignum scientie)*, which was the tree of the mortals. The serpent, in leading Eve and Adam astray, thus deprived man of the eternal life on earth, which was in reality meant for him by the Creator. Despite popular conception, the Bible never mentioned that the Tree of Knowledge was an apple tree. The forbidden fruit was identified only as *"the fruit of the tree which is in the midst of the garden" (The Bible, Old Testament, Genesis III/3).* In the Biblical account of the Temptation, the serpent in the Garden of Eden, or the Garden of the Soul, brought on the fall of man. In the ancient religious beliefs, the serpent was always considered as a male reptile with no higher aspirations than materialism and sensuality; a peculiarly appropriate symbolic representation of Satan, the male personification of all evil. But as early as the 8th century A.D. some artists started to picture in their painted boards, murals, and book illuminations, the serpent that beguiled Eve with the face and bust of a woman; and since that time the Tempter, the satanic male serpent in the Garden is represented everywhere as a female Temptress.

The Biblical Tree of Knowledge, from Meydenbach's
ORTUS SANITATIS, *Mainz, 1491*

THE YGGDRASILL

The Norse mythological world tree, *Yggdrasill* is an evergreen ash tree which overshadows the whole universe. Its roots, trunk and branches bind together Heaven, Earth and the Netherworld. The trunk rooted in the primordial abyss of *Hel*, the subterranean source of matter, bears three stems. The center stem runs up though *Midgard*, the earth, which it supports. It issues out of the mountain *Asgard* where the gods assemble at the base of *Valhalla*. This heaven of the

Yggdrasil, from Finn Magnusen's EDDALAEREN, *Copenhagen, 1824.*

THE YGGDRASILL

Norse heroes can only be reached by *Bifrost,* the bridge of the rainbow. The stem spreads its branches over the entire sky; their leaves are the clouds, their fruits the stars. Four stags, *Dain, Dvalin, Duneyr,* and *Durathor,* which symbolize the cardinal winds, live in these branches, feeding on the flower-buds and dripping dew from their antlers to earth. Upon the top branch perches the eagle, symbol of the air. On its head sits the falcon, *Vedfolnir,* the watchful look-out for the gods. The squirrel, *Batatosk,* signifying rain, snow, hail and the evaporating water, runs up and down the tree, trying to stir up strife between the eagle and the serpent-monster, *Nidhoggr.* The monster, symbolizing the vulcanic powers, gnaws constantly on the roots of the tree, attempting to destroy the earth's foundation. The second stem of the Yggdrasill springs up in *Muspellsheim,* the warm South where the three *Norns: Urth,* the Past, *Verdandi,* the Present and *Skuld,* the Future dwell and the gods sit in judgment. The third stem rises in *Nifleheim,* the cold North, where all the knowledge of mankind flows from the fountain of the Frost-giant, *Mimir,* the personification of Wisdom. The ash tree *(Fraxinus)* itself is the Nordic Tree of Life, symbol of strength and vigor, because the first Norseman *Ask,* sprang from an ash tree according to Norse mythology.

The Ash Tree, from Mattioli's COMMENTAIRES,
Lyons, 1579.

THE ROD OF AARON

When Aaron, the first high priest of the Israelites, and his younger brother Moses were called before Pharaoh, the king demanded a sign of the power of their god. Aaron threw his rod to earth and it became a serpent. Pharaoh's high priest also threw his staff to the ground and it changed into an asp. But Aaron's serpent swallowed the Egyptian's asp and turned back into a rod. *(The Bible, Old Testament, Exodus VII/9-15)*. When Aaron put pressure on the Egyptians to release the Israelites from bondage, he used his rod to start the first three Plagues of Egypt: the conversion of all water into blood, the deluge of frogs and the plague of lice. After the Exodus the rods of the princes of Israel were placed on the Tabernacle to decide which tribe should be the one to furnish the future high priests. It was the staff of Aaron, the Levite, which *budded and brought forth buds and blossomed and yielded almonds,* in token of the valid claim by the tribe of Levy to its exclusive right to the priesthood *(The Bible, Old Testament, Numb. XVII/8)*. In the Dark and Middle Ages, when the professional sorcerers usurped every bit of mythological belief and religious legend of miracles for their own use, they choose the rod of Aaron as the symbol of the magicians' efficacy. The rod became the magic wand for magicians of all times and all peoples.

The Rod of Aaron Blossoming on the Tabernacle, from Arndes' LÜBECKER BIBEL, *Lubeck, 1494.*

THE ACACIA

The acacia tree (*Acacia seyal*) native to Egypt, was called by the Israelites the Shittah-tree. They carried the wood of this tree in their exodus from Egypt through the desert, and later built their Tabernacle and the Arc of the Covenant from this wood to atone for their crime committed at Shittin. The wood of the acacia was considered sacred by the Hebrews, and could not be used for private dwellings, furniture, or any other secular purposes. According to legends of the Near East, when Christ was crowned with thorns as *JESUS NAZARENUS REX JUDAEORUM* — Jesus of Nazareth, King of the Jews, his Roman executioners used the thorny twigs of the acacia, not only to mock its sacredness, but also (which made mockery more complete) because its leaves resembled the ivy with which Kings were crowned. The plant has the mournful distinction of supplying the crown of thorns at Golgatha. Various other plants have been named in different countries as the source of the thorny crown: in Germany, the Holly or *Christdorn* (*Ilex aquifolium*); in France the Hawthorn or *l'épine noble* (*Crataegus oxyacantha*); in Italy the Barberry (*Barberis vulgaris*); in England the Boxthorn (*Lycium sponosum*), the Bramble (*Rubus fruticosus*), or the Buckthorn (*Rhamnus palinurus*). In the Near East where the legend came from, only the acacia was considered to be the provider of the spiny crown.

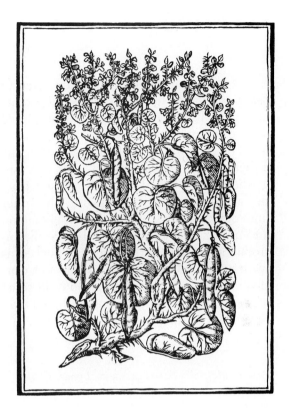

The Acacia, from Mattioli's COMMENTAIRES, *Lyons, 1579.*

The Biblical Crown of Thorns, from an old English Engraving.

THE ACORUS

The acorus is a rush-like plant (*Acorus calamus*), native to the eastern Mediterranean region. In antiquity it was not considered a sacred plant in itself; but the sacred anointment oil of the ancient Hebrews, used at the Tabernacle in Jerusalem, had as its main ingredient the oil of the acorus pressed from the aromatic roots of the plant. The other ingredients were oil of olives, oil of cinnamon and myrrh. In bygone times, before the introduction of carpets, the leaves of the acorus were strewn on the floors of all places of worship. They are still scattered today in some of the churches, temples and cathedrals on festive days.

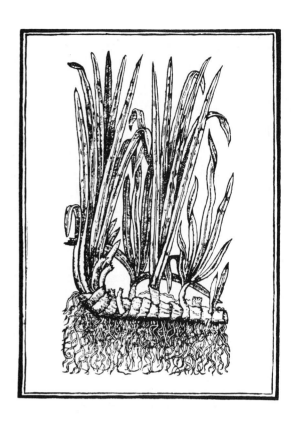

Acorus, Mattioli's COMMENTAIRES, *Lyons, 1579.*

THE BO TREE

The pipal or bo tree (*Ficus religiosa*), native to Hindustan and Ceylon is sacred to Buddha and worshipped by the Buddhists of India. According to tradition it was under a bo tree at Uruvela (today's Bodh-Gaya), Bengal that Buddha sat for seven weeks on a couch of grass facing the East until he obtained the perfect knowledge and enlightment of Nirvana. Today a bo tree grows in every Indian village near the Buddhist temple, surrounded by a mud-platform, on which the meetings and meditations of the villagers are held. Bo trees are exceptionally long lived. The oldest of these trees stands at Amiradapura, Ceylon, and is believed to have been planted in 288 B.C.

Buddha in Meditation under the Bo-tree.

THE CASSIA

The cassia tree *(Cassia cassia)*, native to southern China is an evergreen tree with long cylindrical pods and an aromatic bark with a fragrant, cinnamon-like flavor called Chinese cinnamon, and used as a condiment. According to Chinese religious belief, the cassia tree is considered the sacred Tree of Life. A Chinese mythological legend tells that the celestial World Tree, a cassia tree, has been growing since time immemorial to an incredible height in Paradise, a garden located far up in the Tibetan Mountains at the source of the Hwang-Ho, or Yellow River. Whoever enters Paradise and eats of the fruit of this tree will gain immortality and live happily ever after.

Cassia, Mattioli's COMMENTAIRES, *Lyons, 1579.*

THE CEDAR

The cedar *(Cedrus libana)* is an evergreen tree, growing almost exclusively on the Mountain of Lebanon. There are still many hundreds of these trees growing in the cedar groves of Lebanon, and the twelve oldest and largest are revered by every monotheistic religion; by the Israelites as the Twelve Friends of Solomon, because the Temple of Solomon in ancient Jerusalem was built from cedar-wood; by the Christians as the Twelve Apostles; by the Mohammedans as Saints, and it is believed that an evil fate will overtake anyone who injures one of these trees. Every year at the Feast of the Transfiguration, the Armenians, Greeks and Mormons go on a pilgrimage to the Cedars of Lebanon.

Cedar, Mattioli's COMMENTAIRES, *Lyons, 1579.*

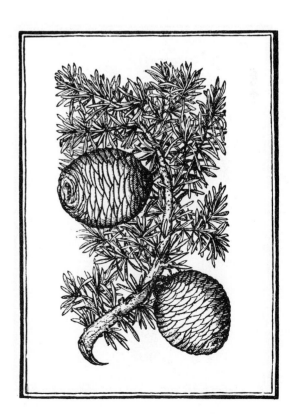

THE DATE PALM

Date Palm and Pond, Symbols of Abundance and Peace, from an Ancient Egyptian Mural.

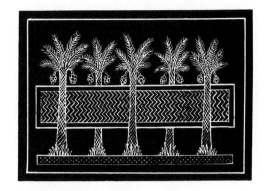

   The date palm *(Phoenix dactylifera)* was one of the most ancient symbolic forms of the Tree of Life in the Near East. Among the Egyptians it was the symbolic Tree of the Year, because it produced a new branch every month. It was the sacred emblem of Judea after the Exodus from Egypt. In the year 53 B.C. the Roman legions took the palm leaf over as the

Fruit-bearing Date Palm, from Mattioli's COMMENTAIRES, *Lyons, 1579.*

THE DATE PALM

emblem of their triumph and victory over Judea, and as a symbol of their plunder and destruction of Jerusalem. In 29 A.D. the Christians accepted the palm leaf as symbolic of the triumphant entry of Christ into Jerusalem. His path was strewn with palm leaves in defiance of the Roman Rulers and the Hebrew hierarchy. The leaves of the palm are still used today as religious symbols by the Christians on Palm Sunday and by the Jews on Passover. In the time of the Catacombs the palm leaf became the emblem of the martyrs, symbolizing the triumph of their faith over their bodies. In the Middle Ages it was believed that the palm tree always grows erect, no matter how it was bent or weighted down; a symbol of triumph over adversity. In the 16th century, a *unicorn's horn* was considered in Europe as an infallible specific for the cure of all diseases. To drink date-palm wine from a unicorn's horn was the best prophylactic against getting sick; a potent healing agent for wounds and burns; and a remedy against poison. In Persia, Arabia and North Africa, the date palm forms one of the principal sources of wealth. In

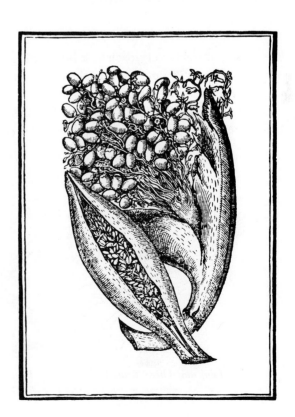

Unripe and Ripening Dates, from Mattioli's COMMENTAIRES, *Lyons, 1579.*

THE DATE PALM

The Unicorn and the Date Palm, from Bock's
KREÜTERBUCH, *Strassburg, 1595.*

the Sahara Desert every oasis is a beautiful garden of date palms. Some Bedouin caravans, or other wanderers of long ago, carelessly dropped the pits of the dried dates which they carried as their only food at their resting place near a well, and in time the treeless oasis became an orchard of life-sustaining date palms. For the nomadic Arabs of today the date palm is still the true Tree of Life because its fruit, fresh or dried, is the main food supply for man and beast.

Palm Leaf and Olive Branch, Symbol of Triumph and Peace, from an Embossing in the early Christian Catacombs.

THE FIG TREE

The common fig tree *(Ficus carica)*, native to the Smyrna region in Asia Minor was one of the most widely revered sacred trees of antiquity. Among the ancient Hebrews the fig tree was a symbol of peace and abundance. It was a sacred tree to the early Christians because Jesus desired to eat figs on the way to Bethany. The Moslems called the fig the Tree of Heaven, and it was considered to be the most intelligent tree, but one step removed from the animal kingdom. It was sacred to the believers of the prophet Mohammed, because according to the Koran, he swore by it. There are several hundreds of species of the fig tree, revered nearly everywhere as the Tree of Life and Knowledge, from Central Africa where the natives believe that the spirits of their ancestors live in fig trees, to the Far East where the Buddhist revere the pipal, a fig tree, because Gautama found wisdom under it. In medieval time the fig was a tree of diversified medical importance. The sap of the tree was used as a purgative and vomative; figs cooked in milk were a remedy for ulcerated gums; boiled in barley water, a relief for pulmonary ailments; and fig juice mixed with bacon drippings, a cure against the bit of mad dogs.

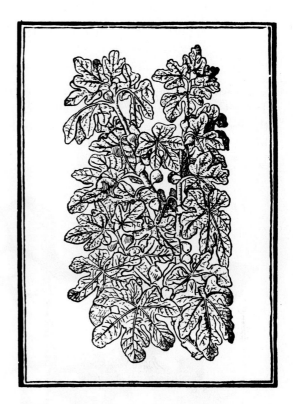

Fig Tree, from Mattioli's COMMENTAIRES, *Lyons, 1579.*

Medicinal Values of the Fig Tree, by D. Kandel, from Bock's KREÜTERBUCH, *Strassburg, 1551.*

THE THREE BLESSED FRUITS

Fu-Shou-San-Tuo, the three blessed fruits, are to the Chinese the revered symbols of the Three Greatest Blessings; the fragrant Hand of Buddha *(Citrus medica)* symbol of happiness; the Peach *(Amygdalus persica)* symbol of longevity; the Pomegranate *(Punica granatum)* symbol of fecundity and a hopeful future.

The Three Blessed Fruits, from a Chinese Lantern Silhouette.

THE THREE BLESSED FRUITS

FO SHOU — BUDDHA'S HAND

Gautama Buddha, resting in the shade of this citrus tree plucked one of its fruit, which was at that time round and bitter tasting. Displeased with its worthlessness, he stretched his hand to make the tree disappear, but in the same instant he took compassion upon it and told the tree that it might live if it would make its fruit pleasing to man. The tree obeyed and changed its fruit to the shape of Buddha's outstretched hand.

TAO — PEACH

The peach tree, called the *Tree of the Fairy Fruit* is presumed to have really originated in China. It is the symbol of immortality because the *Peach Tree of the Gods,* which grew in the mythical gardens of Hsi Wang Mu, the Royal Lady of the West, bloomed only once in 3000 years, yielding 3000 years later the ripened *Fruits of Eternal Life.* This fruit was the sacred food of the Eight Taoist Immortals.

SHI LIU — POMEGRANATE

The pomegranate is not native to China; it was brought there from Kabul, Afghanistan under the Han dynasty in 126 B.C. The ripe and half-open pomegranate, displaying its many seeds, was the symbol of fecundity and eternal life in Semitic antiquity. It also became the Chinese symbol of numerous male offspring rising to fame and glory, and behaving in a virtuous and filial manner. The Buddhists regard its influence as ever and wholly good.

THE LILY

Since time immemorial the lily *(Lilium)* native to the Near East, was the sacred flower of motherhood. It was the symbol of fruitfulness in Sumerian, Babylonian, Assyrian and Egyptian mythology. It was the flower emblem of many chief goddesses of ancient religions. In the pre-historic Minoan period of Crete (3000 B.C.), it was the sacred symbol of Britomartis, also called Dictynna, the Great Mother and Patron of hunters, fishermen, and sailors. In ancient Greece it was the flower of Hera, the goddess of the moon, earth, air, woman's life, marriage and childbirth; and in ancient Rome it was the emblem of Juno, the goddess of light, sky, marriage and motherhood.

Wild Lily, from Mattioli's COMMENTAIRES, *Lyons, 1579.*

The Lily – Symbol of Purity, from an Italian Renaissance Painting, 14th century.

THE LILY

According to ancient Semitic legend, the lily sprang from the tears of Eve, when expelled from the Garden of Eden, she found she was approaching motherhood. In later Christian lore it was said that the lily had been yellow until the day the Virgin Mary stooped to pick it. In Christian symbolism the lily represented purity, chastity and innocence, and is the symbol of resurrection and Easter. The white Madonna lily *(Lilium candidum)* was considered the special flower of the Holy Virgin, and during the Middle Ages it was almost invariably pictured in the subject of the Annunciation placed in a vase standing by the Queen of Heaven.

Madonna Lily, from Schoeffer's HORTUS SANITATIS, *Mainz, 1485.*

The Lily — Symbol of the Virgin Mary, from an old English Manuscript, 15th century.

THE LOTUS

Horus, the Rising Sun on the Lotus Flower, from an Ancient Egyptian Wall Painting.

One of the most revered plants with a deep-rooted, religious significance is the lotus flower, a member of the tropical water lily family *(Nymphaeaceae)*. It is native to many parts of the world; northeastern Africa, Persia, India, Asiatic Russia, China, Japan, southwestern North and Central America. Held sacred by the ancients in the Near and Far East since the beginning of religious beliefs, it has an uninterrupted symbolic history of over 5000 years. The

Anthemion, the Decorative Lotus Frieze of Ancient Greece.

THE LOTUS

Lotus Capital — Symbol of Life, from an Ancient Egyptian Column.

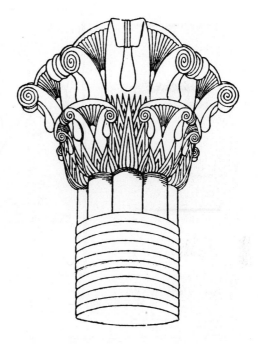

Egyptian lotus, dedicated to Horus, the god of the sun, was the age-old solar symbol of repro-ductive power and fertility since it grew upon the life-giving Nile. Horus was represented in Egyptian mythology issuing from the cup of the lotus blossom, thus signifying immortality and eternal youth. It was also the symbol of resurrection, because the lotus flower closed its petals at night, sinking to the bottom, only to rise above the surface of the water and to open again in

Decorative Lotus Frieze, from Allahabad, India, 250 B.C.

THE LOTUS

Water Lily, from Arnoldi de Nova Villa's TRACTATUS, *Venice, 1499.*

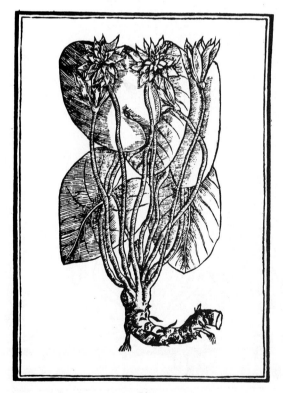

Water Lily, from Mattioli's COMMENTAIRES, *Lyons, 1579*

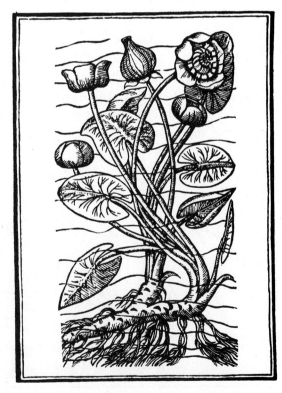

Water Lily, from l'Obel's KRUYDTBOECK, *Antwerp, 1581.*

THE LOTUS

the morning. In antiquity the lotus motif was extensively used as a symbolic ornament in architecture and sculpture along the Mediterranean region: in Assyria it was used as wall decoration; in Egypt in the capitals of columns and wall paintings; and in Greece as anthemion, a frieze ornament derived from the young lotus petals. In Persia the lotus was venerated as the

Lotus Bud, Blossom and Seed-Pod, from a Chinese Lantern Silhouette.

THE LOTUS

The Sacred Lake of Lotuses, from an old Chinese Painting.

THE LOTUS

symbol of the sun and of light; in Hindustan, Nepal, Tatary and Tibet, it was the emblem of mystery. The lotus is revered by all Hindus because Brahma was born in the sacred bosom of the flower, and Hindu deities are pictured seated upon a lotus blossom. The Lama prayer in the praying mills of Tibet and the Himalayas consists of the unceasing repetition of the words *Om-ma-ne pad-me Hum* — "Oh the jewel on the lotus, Amen". The Buddhists in India revered the lotus as the symbol of Buddha, because it sprang up to announce his birth, and in China because it is one of the symbols in Buddha's foot print. The Chinese Buddhists also believe in the so-called Western Heaven with its Sacred Lake of Lotuses, where the souls of the deceased faithful sleep in lotus buds until the appointed time when they are admitted to Paradise. There Buddha resides surrounded by his disciples, while beautiful pavilions float on clouds, precious vases smoke with fragrant incense, music clouds play heavenly melodies, and jewel flowers rain down through the air. The eight-petaled lotus, *Lien* in China, and *Hasu* in Japan, is also the emblem of the Past, the Present and the Future, since buds, blossoms and seed-pods can be

HASU *or* HACHIYO, *the Lotus Flower, Symbol of Paradise, from a Japanese Engraving.*

THE LOTUS

The Birth of Brahma, from an old Hindu Painting.

seen simultaneously on the same plant. The lotus is furthermore considered the symbol of beauty, perfection and purity, because the beautiful blossom grows clean and untouched by the sullied water of the muddy pools from which it rises. Across the Pacific Ocean the water lily, growing in the southwestern part of the North-American continent, and in Central America, was revered by the Mayas as the sacred symbol of the Earth.

Water Lily, Earth Symbol of the Mayans.

THE MISTLETOE

It was common belief in the Dark Ages that mistletoe *(Viscum album)* did not grow from seeds, but from bird droppings, because they grew only high up in trees and never on the ground. Mistletoe was sacred and received the greatest veneration by the ancient Teutonic and Celtic tribes. The Druid priests, after the ceremony of sacrificing a white bull to the good spirits, distributed mistletoe branches among the worshippers. These branches were taken by the people to their dwellings and suspended from the ceiling to ward off all evil spirits. Mistletoe is still used today in many homes at Christmas time, but is banned in churches as a symbol of paganism.

Mistletoe, l'Obel's KRUYDTBOECK, *Antwerp, 1581.*

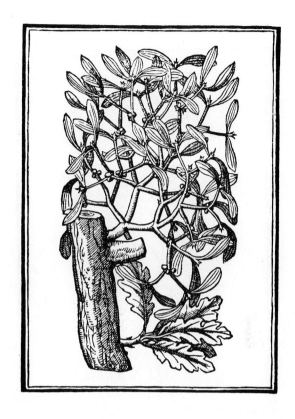

THE MYRTLE

The evergreen myrtle tree *(Myrtus communis)* was in antiquity one of the plants sacred to all peoples around the eastern Mediterranean. It was revered by the ancient Hebrews who covered the tent of their Tabernacle with myrtle boughs in bloom. The Egyptians consecrated it to Hathor, goddess of love, mirth and joy. In Greece and Rome it was sacred to Aphrodite and Venus, the goddesses of love, because when they sprang from the foam of the sea-waves they were preceded by the nereids, carrying garlands of myrtle. The myrtle was considered the symbol of love and marriage, and ever since Roman times brides often wear wreaths of myrtle-blossoms and bridegrooms sprigs of myrtle on the wedding day.

Myrtle, from Mattioli's COMMENTAIRES, *Lyons, 1579.*

THE OAK TREE

Oak Tree, from Mattioli's COMMENTAIRES, *Lyons, 1579.*

Of all the trees in pre-historic times the oak *(Quercus)* was the most widely venerated of all sacred plants because in the mythological belief of many ancient tribes it was the first tree created and man sprang from it. The oak tree was in antiquity sacred to the Hebrews, because Abraham received the angel of Jehovah under its branches; the Greeks dedicated it to Zeus because his oracle in Dodona, an ancient town in Epirus was located in a grove of oaks. To the Romans the oak was the tree of Jupiter; and to the Teutonic tribes, the Tree of Life, sacred to Thor. It was the celestial tree of the Celtic Druids, and no druidic ceremony or rite took place without the aid of the oak tree and its satellite, the mistletoe. The oak tree was also the sacred tree of the pagan Dagda, the Good God and Creator of the ancient Irish Gaels. The fruit of the oak, the lifegiving acorn, main food of the Nordic tribes, became the symbol of fecundity and immortality. With the propagation of agriculture and the rising abundance of cereal grains, the acorn lost its importance as a staple food for humans in northern Europe, and the fruit of the oak tree was relegated to the role of fodder for the pigs.

Swineherd under the Oak Tree, from Bock's KREÜTERBUCH, *Strassburg, 1546.*

THE OXALIS (SHAMROCK)

The shamrock (*Oxalis acetosella*) was an old druidic mystic emblem in Ireland associated as a lucky symbol with the ancient Celtic sun wheel, long before 432 A.D. when St. Patrick arrived to teach Christianity. Its name is derived from the Old Irish *seamair* — clover, and its diminutive *seamrog* — little clover. The Irish legend tells that when St. Patrick, on his missionary journey, preached the doctrine of Trinity for the first time before a powerful chief and his people, the heathen leader asked, *"How can one be three?"*; St. Patrick searching for a simple answer to this question, looked down to the ground and his eye fell on a shamrock plant, the very symbol of the doctrine he was preaching. Stooping down he gathered and upheld before the chief one of the shamrock leaves. *"Here, in this leaf"*, he said, *"three in one, canst thou behold the symbol of my faith, three Gods in One"*. Gazing at the leaf, the old, lucky symbol of the sacred sun wheel, three parts in one, divisible yet indivisible, the chief was impressed. He embraced the new doctrine in his simple heart, and confessing his faith, he was at once baptized by St. Patrick. His people then followed his example. Since then St. Patrick has been the patron saint and the shamrock the national flower of Ireland.

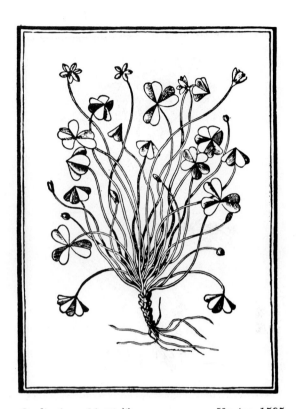

Oxalis, from Mattioli's COMMENTARII, *Venice, 1565.*

Badge of the Most Illustrious Order of St. Patrick, Instituted in 1783.

THE PASSIONFLOWER

The Passionflower, from an old English Engraving.

In the 16th century, when the Jesuits arrived with the conquistadores in South-America they found, to their astonishment, a blooming vine which they believed to be the same flower which according to Christian legend was seen growing upon the cross in one of the many visions of St. Francis of Assissi (1182-1226). The flower was named by the Jesuit Fathers *Flos Passionis* — Passionflower, or *Flor de las cinco llagas*—Flower of the Five Wounds. The floral organs of the passionflower *(Passiflora coerulea)*, are supposed to represent the symbols and instruments of the Passion. In their symbolic meaning the ten petals represent the ten faithful apostles; two are absent because Peter deceived and denied his Lord and Judas betrayed Him. The corona symbolizes the crown of thorns, and the five stamens the five wounds. The ovary signifies the hammer, and the three styles, with their rounded heads, the three nails. The natives who had been cultivating these vines since time immemorial were feasting upon its yellow, egg-like fruits, and the Jesuit Fathers interpreted this as a heavenly sign; that the Indians were hungering for Christianity. They threw themselves with great religious zeal into converting these yearning heathens to Christianity and succeeded in an amazingly short time.

Fanciful Picture of the Passionflower, from Parkinson's PARADISUS, *London, 1629.*

THE PERSEA

The persea tree *(Balanites aegyptica)* also called the bito tree, native to the Near East and Africa is a wild laurel tree growing in the dry regions of Persia and Egypt. It was sacred to the ancient Egyptians, and revered as a symbol of everlasting fame. Thoth, the scribe of the Egyptian gods, deity of science, arts and numbers, recorder of deeds and measurer of time, and Safekh, the goddess of writing, learning and knowledge, inscribed the names and deeds of kings, heroes and high-priests on its leaves, thus securing to them and their names eternal life; a striking equivalent to our Father Time, writing on the symbolic pages of the Book of History.

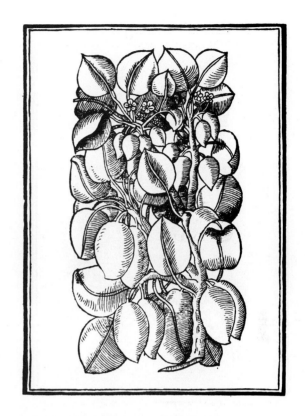

Persea, Mattioli's COMMENTAIRES, *Lyons, 1579.*

The Gods Writing on the Leaves of the Persia Tree, from an Ancient Egyptian Wall Painting

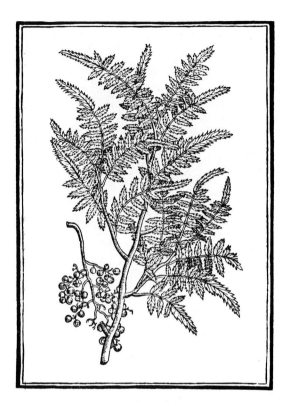

Peruvian Mastic or Molle, from l'Ecluse's SIMPLI-
CIUM MEDICAMENTORUM, *Antwerp, 1579.*

THE PERUVIAN MASTIC

The Peruvian pepper or mastic tree *(Schinus molle)* is a graceful South American shrub, with greenish flowers, succeeded by red, berry-like drupes. The Spanish conquistadores called it *Lentisco del Peru.* This tree, growing in abundance on the plains and hillsides of ancient Peru was sacred to the Incas and their predecessors since antiquity and revered as their most important medicinal tree. The native Indians used every part of it in one form or another as potent medicines. A decoction of its bark was used as a remedy for flatulence, stomach ache, and pain in the groin. An alcoholic, sweet-acid tasting beverage was made from its berries, mixed with honey and vinegar, as a nerve-soothing tonic; an infusion of its crushed leaves, which smelled like fennel, was used as a medicinal tea for relieving pain of any kind. Its manna-like, white resin was of special importance because it was not only used externally in a poultice against inflamed swelling and abscesses, but also cooked in fruit juice and taken internally as a favorite preventive against mistiness of the eyes. It was furthermore believed that the fumes of mastic resin, arising as an incense from hot coals, could drive away torpid tumors.

Peruvian Mastic Tree or Molle, from Durante's
HERBARIO NUOVO, *Rome, 1585.*

THE RESURRECTION FLOWER

The Resurrection plant (*Anastatica hierochuntica*) native to Syria, Arabia and Egypt, was revered by the ancient Hebrews, Christians and Moslems alike. The Jews called it the *Rose of Jericho;* the Christians, the *Rosa-Mariae,* the *Rose of the Virgin,* or the *Resurrection Plant;* and the Moslems, *Kaf Marjam.* According to Christian legend, it sprung up wherever the Holy Family rested in their Flight into Egypt. It is fabled to have blossomed at the Saviour's birth, closed at the Crucifixion and opened again at Easter; whence its name Resurrection Flower. The plant when withered, rolls up into an oval ball, but resumes its original shape whenever it is placed in water or exposed to dampness.

Rose-of-Jericho, Camerarius' HORTUS MEDICUS, *1588.*

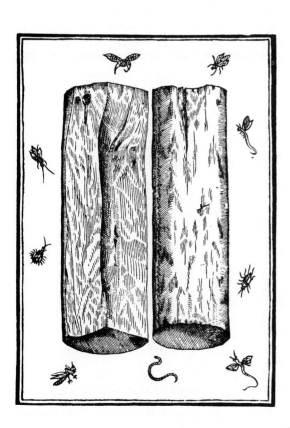

THE SANDALWOOD

The sandalwood (*Santalum album*) native to southern India and the Malay Archipelago, is a parasite tree sending out suckers which attach themselves to the roots of other trees. When the sandalwood dies, its dead log is attacked by termites which destroy all its wood but leave the oily, highly aromatic heart of the trunk intact. This sacred wood, venerated since antiquity by Hindus, Buddhists and and Musselmans, played an important part in religious rituals. It was used for embalming, funeral pyres, and in the construction of temples in India, Burma and China. Sandalwood was introduced to Europe in the 11th century as one of the most precious aromatics of the Far East.

Sandalwood, Jacobus' NEUW KREÜTERBUCH, *1613.*

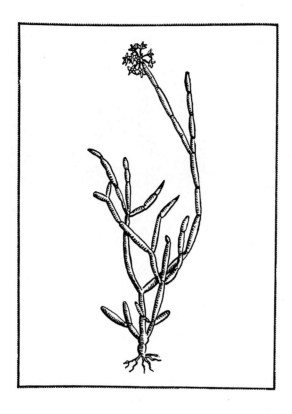

THE SOMA

The leafless soma plant *(Sarcostemma acidum)*, native to East India yields a milky, acidulous, narcotic juice. In ancient India an intoxicating concoction was prepared from its juice by mixing it with buffalo milk, butter, barley and water. This drink was used in Vedic sacrificial rites, in honor of Indra and other Hindu gods. The plant and its juice were considered to have divine power, and were worshiped as the incarnation of Soma, the revered Vedic god of the soma juice, diety of the moon, and lord of the stars and vegetation. Soma, according to ancient Vedic mythology, was born by the churning of the ocean, and occupied the third place among the Vedic gods.

Soma Plant, from an old Oriental Engraving.

THE SUNFLOWER

When Francisco Pizarro in 1532 fought his way into Peru, he found there the giant sunflower *(Helianthus annuus)*, venerated by the Indians of the Inca empire as the sacred image of their sun-god. Incan priestesses, the Maidens of the Sun, wore on their breasts large sunflower disks made of virgin gold. These disks became the most highly treasured spoils of the Spanish conquistadores. Sunflower seeds were also sacred food to the Plains Indians of the prairie regions of North America. They placed ceremonial bowls filled with sunflower seeds on the graves of their dead for food to sustain them on their long and dangerous journey to their Happy Hunting Grounds.

Sunflower, Gerard's HERBALL, *London, 1633.*

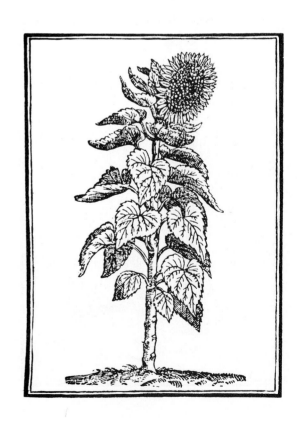

THE SYCAMORE

The wild fig tree of the Scriptures, the sycamore *(Ficus sycamorus)* native to Asia Minor and Egypt resembles the mulberry tree in its leaf and the fig tree in its fruit. Hence: its name was derived from the Greek *sycos* — fig tree, and *moros* — mulberry tree. It was revered in ancient Egypt as the Tree of Life, dedicated to Hathor, the goddess of fertility, love, mirth and joy, and to Nut, the goddess of the underworld, who provided the souls of the dead with drink and nourishment. Every sycamore was an altar to Hathor and Nut; offerings of fruit, grain, vegetables, flowers and water jars were placed at their roots to secure fertility and abundance.

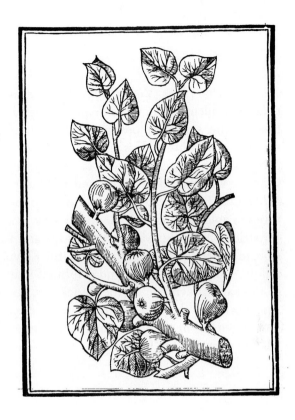

Sycamore, Mattioli's COMMENTAIRES, *Lyons, 1579.*

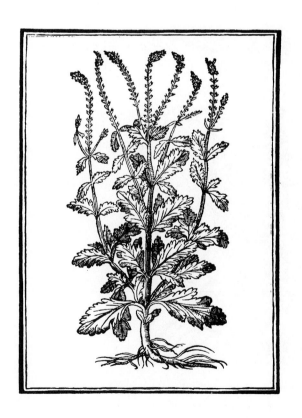

THE VERVAIN

The verbena or vervain *(Verbena officinalis)* was sacred to Mars, the Roman god of war, and its was believed in ancient Rome that the plant had the properties of repelling the enemy. When Roman heralds-in-arms were dispatched to other nations with messages of peace, or to give defiance and challenge to an enemy, they bore crowns of verbena. In ancient Gaul and Britain the plant was held in great veneration, and the Druids who regarded the vervain as a plant of spells and enchantment used it as a sacred food in their rituals. In medieval time the verbena was used for divination, because it possessed the power of warding off witches and enchanters.

Vervain, Mattioli's COMMENTAIRES, *Lyons, 1579.*

THE VINE

The vine plant *(Vitis vinifera)* native to Asia Minor, was one of the Biblical symbols of peace and plenty. The vines in ancient Syria and Judea were trained particularly upon the fig tree, another symbol of peace and abundance. Hence the Biblical proverb: *They shall sit every man under his vine and his fig tree, and none shall make them afraid (The Bible, Old Testament, Micah IV/4)*. It was laid down in the ancient Mosaic law, that in every seventh, or sabbatical year, the vine should not be pruned and the grapes should not be gathered in the vinevards *(The Bible, Old Testament, Leviticus)*. A magnificent reproduction of the vine, its branches sculptured in gold, and its fruit made of precious stones, adorned the eastern wall of the Temple of Jerusalem. After the war against Judea and the capture of Jerusalem in the year 70 A.D., the Roman general and later emperor Titus Flavius Sabinus Vespasianus (40-81 A.D.) carried this unique sculpture to Rome and exhibited it among the spoils of his triumph. The vine was one of the earliest symbols of the Redeemer, according to His own words, spoken by him to the Apostles: *I am the vine; ye are the branches (The Bible, St. John XV/5)*. The vine was used as sacred symbol in the Catacombs, and under Constantine the Great (280-337 A.D.) the first Christian emperor of Rome, it became the sole symbol of the Christian Faith.

Vine; from an antique Byzantine Ceiling Ornament, 6th century.

FLOWER LORE and LEGEND

ONG BEFORE THE human specie roamed the continents of our earth, flowers, plants and trees covered it in luscious abundance. The history of these plants became an inseparable part of the history of mankind. They were around man wherever he ventured: from the door of his dwelling down through the hillsides and valleys to the banks of rivers and the shores of lakes; up through the jungles and forests to the summits of hills and the peaks of mountains. They fed him with their nutritive qualities, healed his wounds and cured his ills with their medical properties, enchanted him with their visual beauty and their fragrant perfumes, and frightened him with their seasonal rising, unfolding and fading away. Man tried with his scientifically untrained power of observation to fathom the why and wherefore behind all these peculiarities. He pondered the occurrences around these plants, and invented scores of tales to explain the inexplainable, so that his searching mind could rest at ease. Many of these legendary tales, sprung from the fertile fantasy of our remote ancestors were handed down in bygone times and believed throughout the centuries. Some are still with us in our own scientific era of research and knowledge.

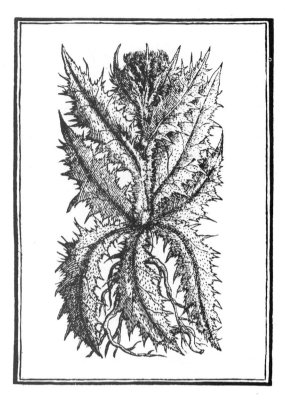

Acanthus, from Mattioli's COMMENTAIRES, *Lyons, 1579.*

THE ACANTHUS

The most beautiful design for the capital of a column that the world has ever seen is the capital of the Corinthian column, patterned after the prickly leaves of the acanthus plant *(Acanthus mollis)* native to the Mediterranean region. Its name is derived from the Greek *akantha* — thorny leaves. The Greek legend tells a story that a young, beautiful girl of Corinth, fell ill and died. After her interment her nurse collected all her trinkets and ornaments, putting them into a basket, which she took to the burial ground. She placed the basket on the tomb, over the roots of an acanthus plant; and lest these trinkets be injured by the weather, she covered the basket with a tile. In spring the acanthus burst forth its stalks and leaves, spreading themselves over the outside of the basket. When they reached the top of the basket they were bent back again by the corners of the tile. The Athenian sculptor and architect Callimachus (5th century B.C.) who happened to pass by the cemetery, was so delighted with the beauty and novelty of this appearance, that he took from it the idea for the capital of the Corinthian column, which he designed. This design then became an architectural monument to an unknown little girl who died 2500 years ago.

Acanthus Motif on the Capital of an Antique Corinthian Column, Greece.

THE ACONITE

The aconite (*Aconitum napellus*) is also called *"monkshood"* from the shape of its flowers. When the Greek hero Hercules in his 12th labor left the Nether Regions in his ascent to the Upper World he was carrying Cerberus, the watch-dog of Hades. The furious animal was spitting venomous froth and wherever a drop of this spittle fell to earth a poisonous plant, the aconite, sprung up. Its juice was used in ancient times as a poison in hunt and war all over Europe and Asia; in antiquity, for poisoning wells and springs to stop advancing armies; in ancient India, to poison arrow-heads for hunting tigers; in France, Germany and Russia to poison bait for wolves.

Monkshood, Mattioli's COMMENTAIRES, *Lyons, 1579.*

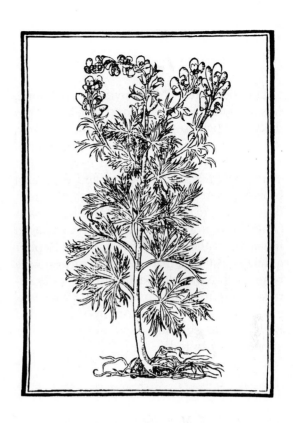

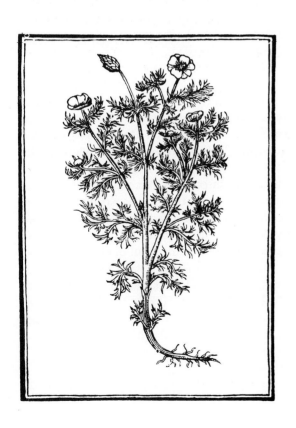

THE ADONIS

The Greek shepherd Adonis was so beautiful that even Aphrodite, the goddess of love and beauty was enamoured by him. Ares, the god of war, became jealous and had Adonis killed at a hunt by a wild boar. Aphrodite's grief was so great that she would not allow the lifeless body to be taken from her arms, until the gods consoled her by decreeing that Adonis might continue half the year on earth, while Aphrodite spent the other half with him in the Nether World. And from the blood-drops of Adonis, mingled with the tears of Aphrodite, sprang the beautiful red adonis-flower *(Flos adonis)*, which reappears on earth every spring and summer.

Adonis, Mattioli's COMMENTAIRES, *Lyons, 1579.*

THE ANEMONE

The beautiful Greek nymph, Anemone, was an attendant at the court of Chloris, the deity of flowers. Chloris' husband, Zephyr, the west-wind, fell in love with the nymph and the jealous Chloris exiled her from her court; where she pined away and died of a broken heart. Zephyr urged Venus, the goddess of love, to change her body into a flower *(Anemone coronaria)*, which always comes to life again at the return of spring. But Zephyr quickly lost interest in this unfortunate beauty and abandoned her to the rude caresses of Boreas, the north-wind, who was unable to gain her love. Annoyed he pulled her blossoms clumsily open and caused her immediately to fade.

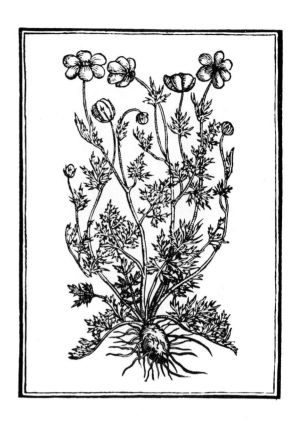

Anemone, Mattioli's COMMENTAIRES, *Lyons, 1579.*

THE CARNATION

The carnation *(Dianthus caryophyllus)* native to the Near East, has been cultivated for the last 2000 years. Its name is derived from the Latin *carnis* — flesh, because the flower is commonly thought of as being pale pink, or flesh-colored. According to Christian legend the carnation appeared on earth the first time when it sprang from the tears shed by Mary on her way to Calvary. The pink carnation became the symbol of mother-love. It was chosen for that reason in 1907 by Ann Jarvis of Philadelphia as the emblem of Mother's Day, observed in the United States as an official holiday on the second Sunday in May to honor motherhood.

Carnation, Lyte's NIEVVE HERBALL, *London, 1578.*

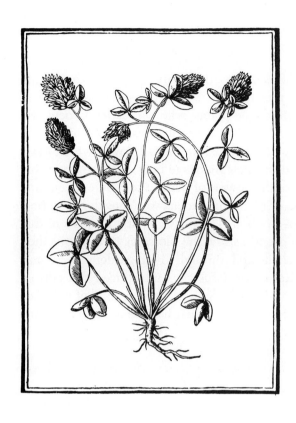

THE CLOVER

The red clover *(Trifolium pratense)* is one of the earliest economic plants cultivated in agricultural countries since antiquity. Highly esteemed not only by the Greeks and Romans, but also by the Celts and Druids, it was always a symbol of good and evil. A five-leaf clover was considered as unlucky; a four-leaf was a good luck charm, which it is still in our time, according to the old folk-rhyme:

One leaf for fame,
And one for wealth,
One for a faithful lover,
And one to bring you glorious health
Are in a four-leaf clover.

Clover, Mattioli's COMMENTAIRES, *Lyons, 1579.*

THE CORNFLOWER

The Greek youth, Cyanus, worshipped Chloris, the deity of flowers. He spent his time gathering cornflowers *(Centaurea cyanus)* for her altars, because he admired this blue flower as the most beautiful of all her gifts. One day Cyanus was found dead in a cornfield, in the midst of a quantity of cornflowers he had gathered. Chloris in token of his veneration for her, transformed his body into the flower he so loved and gave it his name Cyanus. When the Centaur Chiron was one day wounded by an arrow, poisoned with the blood of the Hydra, he covered his wound with cornflowers. This gave it its healing properties and its first name, Centaurea.

Cornflower, Mattioli's COMMENTAIRES, *Lyons, 1579.*

THE CROCUS

The crocuses are a large group of bulbous plants of the iris family, including the saffron *(Crocus sativus)* native to Egypt and the Mediterranean region. According to Greek legend the crocus flower was named after a beautiful youth of the plains, who was called Crocus. He was consumed by the ardor of his unfulfilled love for Smilax, a shepherdess of the hills. Subsequently when Crocus pined away and died, the gods changed him into a flower which bears his name. The ancients often used this flower to adorn their marriage beds because according to the Greek poet Homer, the crocus plant was one of the flowers of which the couch of Zeus and Hera was composed. In ancient Rome at the time of Nero, the crocus was considered to be a great cordial, a tonic for the heart, and a potent love potion. The luxury loving Romans of that time became so fond of the crocus plant that they used to strew the blossoms throughout their banquet halls, fountains and small streams which flowed through their gardens and court yards, filling the air with a beautiful fragrance. Returning Crusaders introduced the saffron-crocus to the table of King Henry I of England (1068-1135), who became very fond of it. When the court ladies started to use up the entire saffron supply to dye their hair, King Henry forbade this use of his favorite spice by severe punishment.

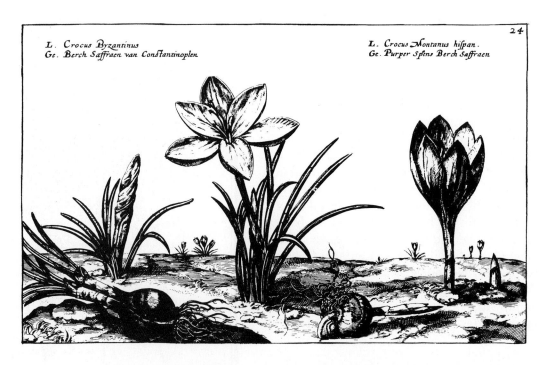

L. *Crocus Byzantinus*
Ge. *Berch Saffraen van Conſtantinoplen*

L. *Crocus Montanus hiſpan.*
Ge. *Purper Spſens Berch Saffraen*

24

Crocus, from De Passe's HORTUS FLORIDUS, *Arnheim, 1614.*

THE CYPRESS

The evergreen cypress tree *(Cupressus sempervirens)*, native to the Himalaya Mountains was introduced into the Mediterranean region by the Phoenicians who in 1,100 B.C. colonized the isle of Cyprus which derived its name from that tree. The Greek poet Ovid (34 B.C.-17 A.D.) tells a mythological legend about the youth Cyparissus, son of Thelephus of Cea, a special friend of Apollo; one day Cyparissus killed by accident a mighty stag, a favorite of Apollo, held sacred by the Dictean nymphs. The youth suffered such agony of remorse for what he had done, that he begged the gods to let his grief endure forever. In answer to his prayers the gods turned him into the cypress tree. The tree became the symbol of the immortal soul and eternal death. In Greek and Roman mythology the cypress was the emblem of the gods of the netherworld, the Fates and the Furies. Its wood was used for Egyptian mummy cases and coffins for Greek heroes because of its proverbial durability, and also because it is not liable to the attacks of insects. Cypresses were planted around cemeteries and at the head of graves. Its branches were carried by mourners at funerals as a symbol of irrevocable death, because the cypress tree, once cut, will never flourish and grow again. To the Western mind, it is a peculiar thought that the cypress tree is a symbol of grace and joy in its native Far East.

Cypress, Mattioli's COMMENTAIRES, *Lyons, 1579.*

THE DAISY

Roman mythological legend informs us that the daisy *(Bellis perennis)* owes its origin to the nymph, Belides, who was one of the Dryads presiding over the forest, meadows and pastures. While dancing one day with other nymphs on the turf on the edge of the forest, she attracted the admiration of Vertumnus, the deity who presided over the orchards. To escape his pursuit she transformed herself into the flower *Bellis*, which is its botanical name. The English name daisy for the bellis-flower is derived from the Anglo-Saxon *daeges eage* — day's eye, from the habit of this flower to close its petals at night and on dark rainy days.

Daisy, Dodoens' PEMPTADES, *Antwerp, 1583.*

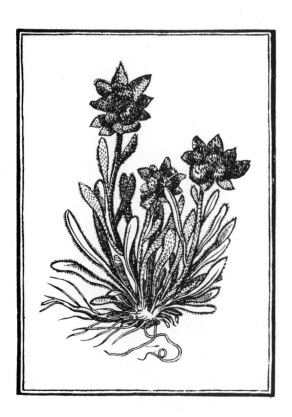

THE EDELWEISS

The edelweiss *(Leontopodium alpinum)* is a little, star-shaped flower with white, velvety leaves native to the Alps, growing high up on the line of perpetual snow, in nearly inaccessible rock crevices. Its German name *Edelweiss* means white jewel. In Alpine countries the gathering of edelweiss is considered an act of daring and a bunch of these flowers brought back from the mountains to a lovely maiden is highly valued by her as proof of the true devotion of her lover. Edelweiss is worn on their hats by mountain climbers, Alpine guides and chamois hunters as a symbol of Alpine achievement. The Edelweiss is the national flower emblem of Switzerland.

Edelweiss, Mattioli's COMMENTAIRES, *Lyons, 1579.*

THE FORGET-ME-NOT

After the Lord had created the Garden of Eden a Christian legend tells that He walked through it and gave every plant a name. He cautioned each plant to be careful not to forget its name, then turned to leave. At this moment He heard the small voice of a diminutive flower at His feet, asking: *"By what name am I called, O Lord?"* And the Lord, struck by His own forgetfulness, smiled down at the frightened little blossom, and said: *"Since I forgot you before, and to remind me never to forget you again, your name shall be Forget-me-not".* And so the forget-me-not (*Myosotis palustris*) became the symbol of remembrance.

Forget-me-not, from an old Engraving, U.S., 1880.

THE HAWTHORN

The hawthorn (*Crataegus oxyacantha*) native to southern Europe, is a small tree of the rose family. Since antiquity it has been considered the emblem of hope, because the Athenian brides used its blossoms to decorate their companions on their nuptial day, while they themselves carried larger boughs of it to the altar. The altar of Hymen, the ancient Greek god of marriage, was lighted by torches made from the wood of this tree; and it also formed the flambeaux which illuminated the nuptial chamber. In ancient Rome the hawthorn was used as a charm against witchcraft and sorcery, and its leaves were put into the cradle of newborn babies.

Hawthorn, Mattoli's COMMENTAIRES, *Lyons, 1579.*

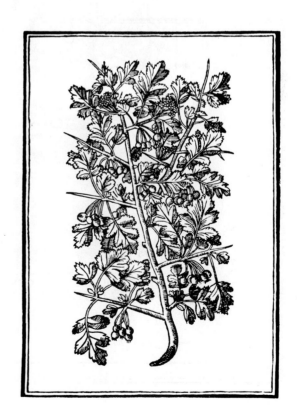

THE HAZELNUT

Apollo, God of Poetry and Music, and Hermes, God of Eloquence, from Moretus' PHILOMATHI
MUSEA IUVENILES, *Antwerp, 1654.*

THE HAZELNUT

The nut-bearing hazel *(Corylus avellana)*, a shrub of Eurasian origin, is a member of the birch family. In Greek mythology the two sons of Jupiter, Apollo, the god of harmony, and Mercury, the god of eloquence exchanged gifts with which they would be impowered to provide a better life for humanity. Apollo received a lyre made of tortoise-shell, whose tone would free the artistic spirit of mankind. Mercury got a winged wand made of hazel; its touch would

The Divining Rod, by Manuel Deutsch, from Agricola's DE RE METALLICA, *Basle, 1556.*

THE HAZELNUT

enable men to express their thoughts by words. The winged hazel rod, entwined with two serpents, became and is still today the symbol of communication, reconciliation and commerce. Among the ancient Romans the hazel was intimately connected with marriage, and it was their custom to burn hazel torches during the wedding night to insure a peaceful and happy union of the newly-wed couple. A rod made from a Y-shaped branch of the hazel was regarded in remote times as having supernatural powers of divination to discover treasures hidden in the bowels of the earth. The supposed art of divining underground riches with a forked branch of hazel, executed since antiquity, was called *rhabdomancy*. This term is derived from the Greek *rhabdos* — rod, and *manteia* — divination. References to such a rod appear in the Bible. The search for water, minerals and ores with a divining rod, *dowsing*, was practised extensively throughout the Dark and Middle Ages and is still used by some prospectors today. In Nordic and Teutonic mythology the hazel was dedicated to Thor, or Donar, the god of thunder, war and strength. In Celtic and Old Irish legend it was the Tree of Wisdom; it represented all human knowledge of the arts and sciences, and was carried by heralds-in-arms on their missions as their official badge of honor.

Hazel, Mattioli's COMMENTAIRES, *Lyons, 1579.*

THE HELIOTROPE

According to Greek mythological legend Phoebus Apollo, the god of the sun, was the lover of the water-nymph, Clytie. When Apollo abandoned her she suffered such grief that she sat on the bank of a river for nine days and nine nights, without food, water or sleep, watching Apollo's chariot from dawn to dusk, waiting at night for the sun to rise again. The gods finally took pity on her and changed her into a flower. They named the flower heliotrope — *the flower which followed the sun,* from the Greek *helios* — sun, and *tropos* — turn. And since that time the heliotrope is considered a symbol of eternal love and admiration.

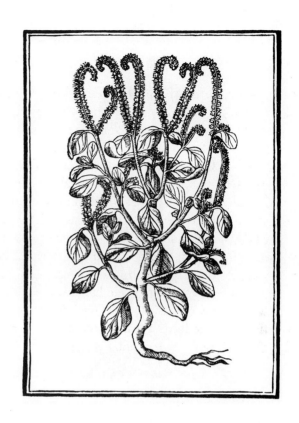

Heliotrope, Mattioli's COMMENTAIRES, *Lyons, 1579*

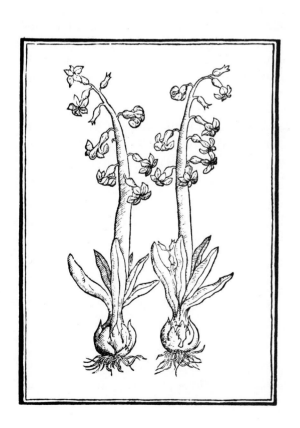

THE HYACINTH

In Greek mythological legend, Hyacinthus, a beautiful Laconian youth was beloved by Apollo, the sun-god, and by Zephyrus, the west-wind. One day Hyacinthus matched Apollo in a game of quoits, a sport akin to horseshoe pitching, where flat metal rings were thrown over a peg. The jealous Zephyrus blew a quoit thrown by Apollo from its course, and the heavy ring smote Hyacinthus on the head and killed him. The grieved Apollo changed the blooddrops of his dead friend into the beautiful flower Hyacinth *(Hyacinthus).* Symbolizing the vegetation scorched by the hot disc of the summer sun and its resurrection in spring, this legend was commemorated in ancient Greece in the yearly *Hyacinthia* festival.

Hyacinth, Mattioli's COMMENTAIRES, *Lyons, 1579.*

THE IRIS

Florentine Iris, Mattioli's COMMENTAIRES, *Lyons, 1579.*

The iris *(Iris florentina),* native to the Mediterranean region and southern Europe, was considered by the ancient Egyptians as a symbol of power and placed on the brow of the Sphinx. It was placed throughout the centuries on the sceptors of kings and rulers, because the three large petals of the iris symbolized faith, wisdom and valor. This multicolored flower was named after Iris, the Greek goddess of the multicolored rainbow, the swift-footed messenger of Zeus and Hera. The Greeks planted irises on the graves of women, because one of the duties of Iris was that of leading the souls of dead women to the Elysian Fields. According to French historical lore, the iris was the flower symbol of Gaul as far back as the 1st century A.D. When Clovis I, King of the Franks, and founder of the Merovingian dynasty, defeated the Alemanni in the Battle of Tolbiac (496 A.D.) his victorious soldiers crowned themselves with irises blooming near the battle-field. But not before the time of Charles IV (1294-1328) did the iris adorn the banner of France. The name fleur-de-lis was derived from Löys, in which manner the first twelve Louis, kings of France, up to Louis the XII (1462-1515) signed their name.

Fleur-de-Lis, Emblem of France, from a 15th century Engraving.

THE IVY

The ivy plant *(Hedera helix)* is an ever-green, clinging vine native to Europe and Asia. In ancient Greece it was called *cissos* because, according to a mythological legend it was named after the nymph, Cissos, who at a feast of the gods, danced with such joy and abandon before Dionysus that she fell dead from exhaustion at his feet. Dionysus was so moved by her performance and untimely death, that he turned her body into the ivy, a plant which graciously and joyfully en-twines and embraces everything near it. The ivy, dedicated to the wine-god Dionysus, is hung even today in wreathes over the doors of taverns and wine-shops.

Ivy, Gerard's HERBALL, *London, 1633.*

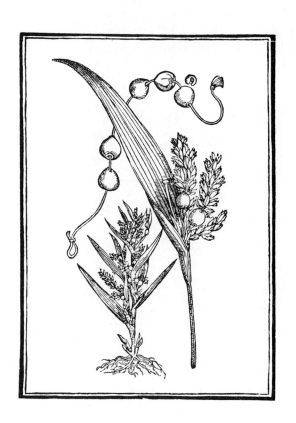

THE TEARS OF JOB

Job's tears *(Coix lacryma-jobi)*, native to India, is a relative of the maize plant. Its name is derived from the fanciful resem-blance between its gleaming pearl-white seeds and the appearance of tear-drops as they fall sparkling from the eye. According to Christian legend it was imagined that the plant grew from the tears of Job, whose pro-verbial sufferings and troubles did not make him lose his faith in God *(The Bible, Old Tes-tament, Book of Job)*. These beadlike seeds, staple food to the hill tribes of India, medi-cine to the Chinese, were used for rosaries in the Near East and for magic necklaces in ancient Persia.

Jobs tears, Simler's VITA GESNERI, *Zurich, 1566*

THE LAUREL

Apollo and Daphne, by Jacobo Ripanda Bolognese, Rome, 1500.

THE LAUREL

The Greek nymph Daphne, daughter of the river-god Peneus, was one of the attendants of Athene, goddess of wisdom, skill and war. One day she was pursued by Apollo and in her flight she prayed to the gods that the earth would yawn and swallow her or else change her form which caused her to be the prey of her pursuer. Her prayers were answered, and at the point of being overtaken by Apollo, Athene transformed her into the laurel tree *(Daphne laureola)*. Apollo chose the laurel tree as his favorite personal tree, and as an evergreen with intoxicating properties it symbolized poetic inspiration and immortal fame. It was believed in antiquity that the laurel endowed prophets with vision, and the Pythian priestess at Delphi, the oracle dedicated to Apollo, chewed laurel leaves to induce oracular powers. The victors in the Pythian Games held at Delphi at the end of every fourth year since the 7th century B.C. in honor of Apollo, the slayer of the serpent Python, were crowned with laurel for their achievements in music, poetry, painting, sculpture, athletic sports, chariot and horse racing. And a crown of leaves from the laurel tree signifying a special distinction for outstanding performance and victory, became the ambition and reward of every poet, painter, sculptor, musician, orator, philosopher, soldier, ruler and athlete from the time of ancient Greece and Rome to its symbolic presentation in our time.

Laurel, Mattioli's COMMENTAIRES, *Lyons, 1579.*

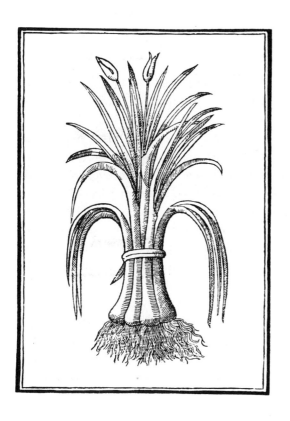

THE LEEK

The leek *(Allium porrum)* was revered in antiquity, because a man with leek on him was sure to be victorious in every fight and suffer no wounds. It was the custom in ancient Wales, for every farmer to contribute his leek to the common repast when they met at the *cymmortha* or association formed for reciprocal assistance in ploughing their land. The legend tells that when the Saxons invaded Wales in the 6th century A.D. St. David, patron saint of Wales, directed the Britons to wear leek on their caps, to distinguish them from the enemy. In memory of the heroic resistance by the Britons, the leek became the national emblem of Wales.

Leek, Mattioli's COMMENTAIRES, *Lyons, 1579.*

THE LILY-OF-THE-VALLEY

According to a French legend, there lived in 559 A.D. in the forest of the Vienne Valley, near Limoges, a holy man known as St. Leonard. Having renounced all wordly things, he lived the life of a hermit in the depths of the woods. The dragon Temptation also dwelled there and terrible combats took place between them. The dragon was driven further and further back toward the edge of the forest, until it finally disappeared altogether, leaving the hermit the conquerer. The places of their battles were marked by beds of lilies-of-the-valley *(Convallaria majalis)* which sprang up wherever the ground was sprinkled with the blood of St. Leonard.

Lily-of-the-Valley, COMMENTAIRES, *Lyons, 1579.*

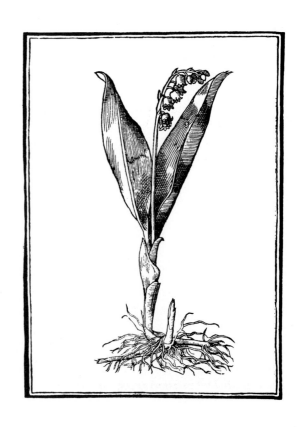

THE LINDEN TREE

In the Greek legend of Philemon and Baucis, the classical Phrygian couple of wedded love were allowed by Zeus to die at the same moment and their bodies were metamorphosed into trees: Philemon into an oak, the symbol of hospitality, and Baucis into a linden, ever since the emblem of conjugal love. Beauty, grace and simplicity, an extreme softness of manners, and an innocent gaiety are the properties and accomplishments of a tender wife. All these qualities can be found united in the linden, which in the spring is covered with a soft delicate verdure. It exhales a delightful fragrance, while it lavishes the honey of its blossoms upon the busy bees. The linden or lime tree (*Tilia*) was the ancient emblem tree of Germanic countries eulogized by the *Bards* and *Meistersinger* in their ballads and rhymes. Every hamlet in Germany has its official town-linden on the main square, some planted 1,000 years ago. Since uncounted time the village people, old and young, gather on warm summer evenings under the linden, to gossip, to dance or to romance. Its name is derived from the Latin *lentus* — flexible, lithe, because the smooth, pliable bast of its bark was used in antiquity, and is still used today for binding creeper plants, as hop or vines to posts and poles without bruising them.

Linden or Lime Tree, from Jacobus' NEUW KREÜTERBUCH, *Frankfort, M., 1613.*

Villagers Dancing under the Linden, from Bock's KREÜTERBUCH, *Strassburg, 1546.*

THE MULBERRY TREE

Pyramus and Thisbe, from Boccaccio's GÉNÉALOGIE DES DIEUX, *Paris, 1498.*

THE MULBERRY TREE

An ancient Babylonian legend tells of Pyramus and Thisbe, a handsome youth and a lovely maiden who had lived in adjoining houses from early childhood. The two always played together and after they grew up they fell in love. Their parents in the meantime had quarreled bitterly over some trifles and forbade their union. But the two lovers found a chink in the wall dividing the two houses, and every night when everybody else was asleep, they whispered sweet words to each other through the crack in the wall until dawn. One night they agreed to meet on the coming night of the full moon outside the city under a white mulberry tree which stood near a bubbling spring close to the tomb of Ninus, the founder of Nineveh and husband of Semiramis. Thisbe, who arrived first, encountered a lion who had just killed an ox. She fled in terror dropping her veil, which the lion bloodied up while tearing it to pieces. When Pyramus arrived later he found the torn, bloody garment, and believing Thisbe dead, killed himself with his own dagger. The returning Thisbe found her dying lover under the mulberry tree, and in her grief plunged his dagger in her own heart. The mingling blood of the two unhappy lovers spurted over the mulberry tree, coloring its fruit, and the mulberry tree *(Morus rubra)* has ever since born blood-red fruit.

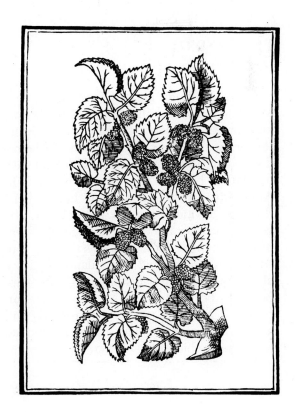

Red Mulberry or Silkworm Tree, from Mattioli'
COMMENTAIRES, *Lyons, 1579.*

THE MULLEIN

The mullein *(Verbascum thapsus),* native to Europe, was also called the torch flower because the soldiers of the Roman legions who remained in conquered Central Europe used to dip this plant in tallow to make torches for their billets. The thick down of the mullein is still used to make candle wicks in some parts of Europe. In medieval times the plant was also known as the flannel flower because of the fact that its stems and leaves were covered with this downy wool. It was considered a potent charm against demons and also regarded as a love herb, because it was used by witches and warlocks as an integral part of their brews and love potions.

Mullein, Gerard's HERBALL, *London, 1633.*

THE MYRRH

According to an ancient Oriental legend, Myrrha or Smyrna, the daughter of Theias, king of Assyria, was caused by Aphrodite, the Oriental goddess of vegetation and reproduction to commit an incestuous love act with her father because she refused to worship Aphrodite. Myrrha fled from her father's drunken advances and to protect her, the gods turned her into the myrrh shrub *(Commiphora myrrha).* The true myrrh, native to Arabia, Abyssinia and Somaliland exudes a clear, fragrant, bitter-tasting gum resin, supposed to be the tears of Myrrha. Since antiquity it has been used as an aromatic and a stimulating tonic. The name is derived from the Arabic *Mur* — bitter.

Myrrh, Pomet's HISTORY OF DRUGGS, *London, 1725.*

THE NARCISSUS

Narcissus, a beautiful, young Greek semi-deity, the son of the river-god, Cephissus and the nymph Liriope, was pampered so much in his early youth by all the nymphs, that he became the personification of egotism and self-conceit. The beautiful mountain nymph Echo, one of the servants of Hera, fell in love with Narcissus but her affection was not returned by him. He idled all his waking hours on the brink of fountains and springs, gazing enchanted at the reflection of his own face in the crystal-clear waters, because it so closely resembled the sister he had lost. He fell deeper and deeper in love with himself. The unfortunate, grieving Echo wasted away until only her voice remained. The voice ran off into the mountains to mock every other voice it heard. Hera became so enraged by the conceited behavior of Narcissus that she ordered Nemesis, the deity of vengeance, to punish him for his egotism. Nemesis changed the youth into the narcissus flower (*Narcissus poeticus*) so he could stand along the waters nodding at his own image for time eternal. The Fates wore wreaths of narcissus flowers, the scent of which was so painfully sweet as to cause madness, a reminder that narcissism, the symbol of egotism and conceit, will be punished in the end.

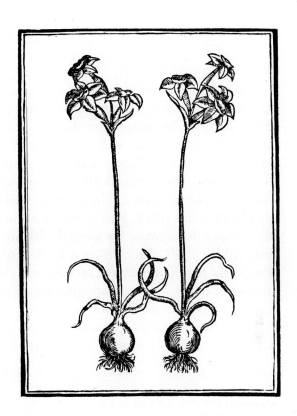

Narcissus, from Mattioli's COMMENTAIRES, *Lyons, 1579.*

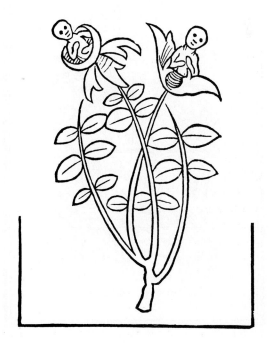

Fanciful Picture of the Narcissus, from Meydenbach's ORTUS SANITATIS, *Mainz, 1491.*

THE OLIVE TREE

Asia Minor is credited with being the original home of one of the oldest fruit trees known to man, the olive tree *(Olea europaea)*. This evergreen tree was cultivated in the Near East and the Eastern Mediterranan since the Neolithic Age. Olives remained one of the chief staples of husbandry and trade since the early days of Minoan Crete (3,000 B.C.). The olive was carried from there to Greece, Rome, Gaul and Spain, and the Spanish brought it to the Americas. In Greek legend, Poseidon and Athene disputed after whom the nameless, newly founded city of Athens should be named. The gods decided that the one who gave the best gift to mankind should have this honor. Poseidon struck the seashore with his trident and there sprang forth the horse; Athene smote the ground with her spear and the olive tree arose. The gods decreed that Athene's gift, the olive as a symbol of peace, was infinitely better for humanity than Poseidon's horse, an emblem of war; and the new city was named Athens. The olive is the symbol of peace, because barbaric tribes conceding defeat and asking for peace, sent an olive branch to the victors. It is a token of safe travel because Noah's dove brought back an olive branch from the Ararat Mountain; it is an emblem of achievement because the victors in the Olympian Games were crowned with an olive wreath.

Olive Tree, from Mattioli's COMMENTAIRES, *Lyons,*
1579.

THE ORANGE TREE

The orange is not a fruit, but a berry of the orange tree *(Citrus sinensis)* native to the Far East. Its English name is derived from the Sanscrit *narange* — orange. According to Greek mythological belief, the golden apple presented by Gaea, the ancient goddess of the earth and fertility as a wedding-gift to Hera on the day she married Zeus, was an orange. The Golden Apples of the Hesperides, grown from the seeds of that fruit, were the orange trees. In the 11th century the Moors introduced the bitter orange tree of the East into Spain. Under their regime, up to the 15th century, no *giaour*, or unbeliever in the Iberian Peninsula was allowed under pain of death, to eat an orange or to drink its juice, before embracing the Mussulmanic faith. The custom of using orange blossoms for bridal fashions dates back to the Crusaders, who saw the Saracen brides wear orange blossoms on their wedding day as a symbol of fecundity, because the orange was a prolific fruit-bearing plant. The blossoms represented an appeal to the orange tree spirit that the bride should not be barren. Throughout the centuries the use of orange blossoms as bridal flowers was adopted in all of southern and western Europe, England and on the continent of North America.

Orange Tree, from Mattioli's COMMENTAIRES, *Lyons, 1579.*

The Golden Apples of the Hesperides, from an Antique Greek Vase Painting.

THE PLANE TREE

The plane tree *(Plantanus occidentalis)* was the symbol of genius in ancient Athens because the Greek philosophers held their studies and discourses under its wide-spreading shade. When Xerxes, King of Persia, crossed the Hellespont in 480 B.C., he saw his first plane tree. So attracted by its charm was he that he caused his army of 1,000,000 men to halt. He adorned the tree with all his jewels, with those of all his concubines and of the lords of his court, until the branches were loaded with ornaments of every kind. He declared the tree his goddess and mistress, and was persuaded only with great difficulty to leave the tree of which he had become so enamoured.

Plane Tree, Mattioli's COMMENTAIRES, *Lyons, 1579.*

THE BLACK POPLAR

The black poplar tree *(Populas nigra)* was consecrated in Greek antiquity to Hercules, who according to mythological legend, wore a crown of its foliage when he descended to the Gates of Hades to bring Cerberus up to earth in his 12th labor. The fable has it that the black poplar leaf is a different shade on each side for this reason: when Hercules donned his crown of poplar leaves the sweat of his brow moistened one side of the leaves and they retained their natural color. But the other side, exposed to the smoke and vapor of the infernal regions he visited were tinged by the dark shade which they still retain today.

Black Poplar, Mattioli's COMMENTAIRES, *1579.*

THE ROSE

Rose, from Macer's VIRIBUS HERBARUM, *Naples, 1477.*

The most beautiful member of the *Rosaceae family;* the rose *(Rosa)* originated in Asia Minor and is one of the oldest flowers in cultivation. It was grown 5,000 years ago in the ancient gardens of western Asia and north-eastern Africa. Roses have been mentioned in every poetical work since the dawn of civilization, from the Biblical *Rose of Sharon* in the Songs of Solomon, to the Garden of Roses, *Gulistan,* in the work of the Persian 13th century poet Muslih-ud-Din Sâdi. Roses grew in the mythical gardens of Semiramis, queen of Assyria, and Midas, King of

The Red Rose of Lancaster, the White Rose of York, and the Red and White United Rose of Tudor, from Parker's Annales of England, Oxford, 1855-57.

THE ROSE

Phrygia. Every mythological belief assigned the rose as the symbolic emblem of beauty, youth and love. According to Greek mythological legend, Chloris, the deity of flowers, one cloudy morning walked through the woods and found the body of a beautiful nymph. Saddened to see such a lovely creature dead she decided to give her new life by transforming her into a beautiful flower surpassing all others in charm and beauty. She called on the other deities to help her with her task: Aphrodite, to give beauty; the three Graces, to bestow brilliance, joy and charm; her husband, Zephyrus, the West-wind, to blow away the clouds so that Apollo, the Sun, could send his blessing through his rays: and Dionysius, the deity of wine, to give nectar and fragrance. When the new flower was finished, the gods rejoiced over its charming beauty and delicate scent. Chloris collected a diadem of dewdrops and crowned the new flower, the rose, as the queen of all flowers. Aphrodite presented the rose to her son, Eros, the deity of love. The white rose became the symbol of charm and innocence, and the red rose of love and desire. When Eros in turn gave the rose to Harpocrates, the deity of silence, to induce him to conceal the weaknesses of the gods, the rose became the emblem of silence and secrecy. In ancient times a rose was attached to the ceiling of council chambers as an indication that everybody

Damask Rose, from Mattioli's COMMENTAIRES,
Lyons, 1579.

THE ROSE

present was sworn to secrecy, *sub rosa* — under the rose. The *rosette* sometimes decorating the center of the ceiling of our rooms·today is an unconscious use of this ancient symbol of secrecy. *Attar,* the oil of the damask rose, *Rosaceum,* an ointment of rose oil and honey, and rose water were the most lavishly used perfumes and cosmetics in ancient Persia, Egypt, Greece and Rome. According to an old Persian legend, the caliph Jehangir, while walking with his beautiful bride in his palace gardens along the canals and fountains, decked with rose petals in celebration of their wedding, noticed an oily film on the surface of the waters, produced by the action of the sun on the roses. Fascinated by the heavy scent of this oil he ordered it bottled for later use. And this attar of roses — from the Persian *atar* — fragrance was considered henceforth the most precious of all Persian perfumes. The rose became one of the most prominent heraldic flowers in history since the so-called *War of Roses* (1455-1485), fought between the House of York, whose emblem was the white rose, and the House of Lancaster, with the red rose as its badge. The war ended with the establishment of the House of Tudor on the English throne. The Rose of Tudor, a white rose charged upon a red one is today the flower emblem of England.

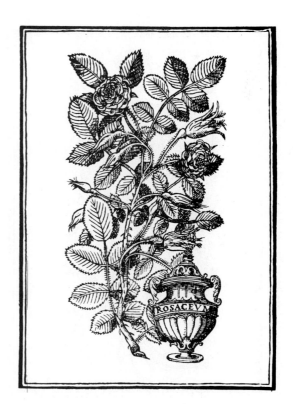

Rosaceum or Unguent of Rose-oil, from Mattioli's COMMENTAIRES, *Lyons, 1579.*

THE SYLPHIUM

The sylphium was a North-African plant discovered in the mountains of Cyrene in the 6th century B.C. during the reign of King Arcesilas. The plant became one of the main sources of *Frankincense*, a fragrant gum resin used extensively in ancient Egypt and Asia Minor as a medical cure-all, and for embalming and fumigation. The kingdom of Cyrene became the prosperous Greek colony Cyrenaica (Lybia) with frankincense its main export article. Over-exploited as a source of wealth for the colony, the sylphium plant became extinct about the time of Christ. Only stylized pictures of the vanished plant could be found on old Cyrenean coins (500 B.C.).

Sylphium, from a Cyrenean coin, 600 B.C.

THE THISTLE

The common white cotton thistle or Scotch thistle *(Onopordon acanthium)* is a plant of Eurasian origin. According to Scotch legend, the Norsemen invaded Scotland during the reign of Malcolm I (938-958 A.D.) and beleaguered Staines Castle. One night the Norsemen took off their footgear to wade the moat, only to find it dry and filled with cotton thistles. Their painful yells and curses roused the garrison and the Norsemen were soundly defeated. In memory of this victory the thistle became the flower emblem of Scotland. In 1687 James VII founded the Most Noble and Most Ancient Order of the Thistle of Scotland, also called the Order of St. Anthony.

Cotton Thistle, Gerard's HERBALL, *London, 1633.*

THE TULIP

The tulip *(Tulipa)* is a wild-flower of Persian origin. An Oriental legend tells that a Persian youth, Ferhad, became enamoured of the maiden Shirin who rejected his love. Ferhad went out into the desert to die of a broken heart. As he wept there for his lost love and pined away, every tear falling into the barren sand turned into a beautiful blossom. These flowers, called *lalé* in Persian became the symbol of the Perfect Lover. In 1500 tulips were extensively cultivated in Turkey, and because of their resemblance to the Turkish *tulbend* — turban, were called *tulipam,* and became the emblem of the ruling House of Osman. In 1554 Ogier Ghiselin de Busbecq, ambassador of Emperor Ferdinand I to Sultan Suleiman the Magnificent, brought the first tulips to Vienna. In 1561 the herbalist, Konrad Gessner, was commissioned by the merchant-princes of the House of Fugger to bring tulip-bulbs from the Levante to Augsburg. He published the first printed picture of a tulip in his herbal. In 1562 the first bulbs from Constantinople reached Antwerp by ship and the ensuing craze for growing tulips in Holland (the Tulipomania), ended in financial disaster for that country. After the Dutch government enforced strict laws for the cultivation and sale of tulip-bulbs, the flower became the national emblem of Holland.

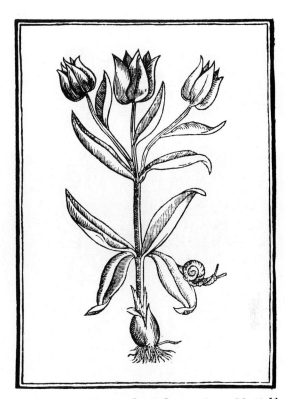

LALÉ *or Constantinople Tulipam, from Mattioli's* COMMENTAIRES, *Lyons, 1579.*

The First Printed Picture of a Tulip, from Gesner's DE HORTIS GERMANIAE, *Basle, 1561.*

THE VIOLET

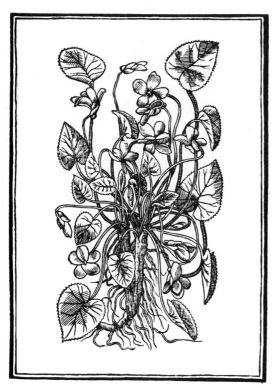

Violets, from Mattioli's COMMENTAIRES, *Lyons, 1579.*

A Greek mythological legend relates that the nymph Io, daughter of the river-god Inachus was beloved by Zeus. To hide her from the suspicious eyes of Hera, he changed her into a white heifer. When Io shed tears over the coarseness of the common grass she was forced to feed on, Zeus decide to create a new and more suitable plant for the delicate creature. He changed her tears into a sweet-smelling, dainty flower, the violet *(Viola odorata)* as a special feed for Io. The violet is one of the few flowers which entered the historical arena as a political symbol. In the year 1814 during the exile of Napoleon I at Elba, the French Bonapartists chose the violet, the flower of March, as their emblem because the Capitulation of Paris, preceding Napoleon's abdication, occurred on March 30. Napoleon was nicknamed *Caporal Violet, the little flower that returns with Spring.* France was soon flooded with postcards picturing a bunch of innocent looking violets. But a little scrutiny revealed in the bouquet of violets, the outlines of portraits of Napoleon, Maria Louise and of their three year old son Charles, King of Rome. On and off until the year 1874, the French governments fought by decree any reproduction showing a violet, the symbol of the Bonapartists.

Bunch of Violets Containing the Silhouettes of Napoleon I, Empress Louise and the King of Rome. Picture Card Circulated in France, 1815.

STRANGE and WONDROUS PLANTS

REEK AND ROMAN mythology, coupled with the beliefs and religions of Occidental and Oriental antiquity have bequeathed to us many a poetic and charming legend of flowers, plants and trees. It took the gloomy ignorance of the Dark and Middle Ages, when the people of the Western World believed in dragons and demons, satanic and magic powers, witches' brews and sorcerers' potions, to provide us with wild and weird stories of strange and wondrous plants. In these days when distances were far and voyages slow, adventurers and traders, mariners and travellers, returning from far away places brought back tales about real and imaginary plants of fantastic shapes and strange behavior, and of mystic virtues and magic powers. Scientists and herbalists pondered over the truth of these stories and reported on some of these wondrous plants and their peculiarities in their herbals and natural histories. Sometimes the reports were illustrated according to a description and explanation by untrained observers who had seen the plants or merely heard about them. After many centuries of painstaking research and broadened knowledge, some of these tales were found to be reality, but many were discarded as fantastic exaggeration or plain fabrication, and were quickly forgotten in the following centuries.

THE APPLE OF SODOM

Ancient travellers and writers returning from Asia Minor to Europe told that they saw a peculiar and mysterious fruit, called the Apple of Sodom, growing at the site of the Biblical twin-cities Sodom and Gomorrah, which were destroyed by the Lord through fire from heaven because of the sinful wickedness, vice and corruption of their inhabitants: *"The Lord rained upon Sodom and upon Gomorrah brimstone and fire from the Lord out of heaven" (The Bible, Old Testament, Genesis XIX/24).* They say in these bygone times that the plant was reputed to lure weary, thirsty and hungry travellers with the luscious appearance of its fruit which resembled edible apples in form and color. However at the very moment the fruit was touched by human hands it immediately turned into smoke and ashes, as a warning and symbolic reminder of the destruction of Sodom and Gomorrah. In reality the fruit may have been subject to the attack of an insect which left the rind untouched while the interior became mere rot and dust. Today the name of Apple of Sodom or Dead Sea Fruit, is given to a shrub of the nightshade family *(Solanum sodomeum)* growing on the arid shores of the Dead Sea, an inland body of salt water between Palestine and Trans-Jordan. The fruit of this plant, related to the eggplant, and resembling a small, yellow tomato is poisonous and is considered the symbol of sin in the Near East.

Dead Sea Apples, from Maundevile's VOIAGE AND TRAVAILE, *London, 1725.*

THE AMBER TREE

Amber is a yellow or brownish, translucent, fossilized resin from prehistoric evergreen trees. It has been used since antiquity for magic purposes and talismanic jewelry. Because it was found on the shores of the sea, on the banks of great streams, and in dried up river-beds, the naturalists of bygone times could not make up their minds if amber were mineral, animal, or vegetable. The herbalists in the 15th century could still not decide whether amber was crystalized sea-foam, the product of the amber-fish, or the fruit of the amber-tree. But they leaned more and more to the belief that it was the petrified gum of a tree, which it really is.

Amber Tree, Meydenbach's ortus sanitatis, *1491.*

THE BAUSOR TREE

Medieval travellers returning from the Far East told tales about a fabulous Malayan tree growing on the isles around *Cathay* (China), called *Bohun Upas* — Tree of Poison. It was considered a symbol of death because it was believed that it exhaled narcotic fumes, which not only destroyed all vegetation within a radius of many yards, but also killed any animal or person that rested and fell asleep under it. Prisoners were executed by tying them to these trees. Today there are still upas-trees *(Antiaris toxicaris)* found in Java, Malaya and the Philippines. They are supposed to be the descendants of the legendary bausor-tree whose milky juice the natives used as arrow-poison.

Bausor Tree, Meydenbach's ortus sanitatis, *1491.*

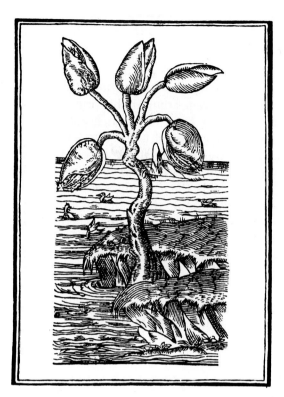

THE BREEDE OF BARNAKLES, *from Gerard's* HERBALL, *London, 1597.*

THE BARNACLE TREE

The origin of the migrating wild geese coming from the North was for a long time a deep mystery. It was a common belief in 15th century Europe, that the barnacle goose *(Branta bernicla),* breeding in the Far North, grew on trees. These goose-trees, or barnacle-trees, according to old mariner's yarns, were growing somewhere north of Scotland on the shores of the Orcades (Orkney Islands). As fruit they bore barnacles. When these barnacles were ripe they fell into the sea and developed into barnacle-geese. This belief was based on the appearance of the goose barnacles, which attached themselves to rocks, submerged logs, or the bottoms of ships. They looked astoundingly like embryonic geese. Renowned botanists and zoologists in the 16th century reported and discussed earnestly the stories about the goose trees and the barnacle geese. Some of the scientists took the existence of these trees for granted and included these specimens in their herbals. John Gerard in his *Herball or Generall Historie of Plants* (1597) published a fanciful picture of the *Breede of Barnackle-geese.* Today, centuries after the belief in these fantastic sailor yarns of tree-grown geese has been shattered and forgotten, the official scientific terms *barnacle goose* and *goose barnacle* are still used in zoology.

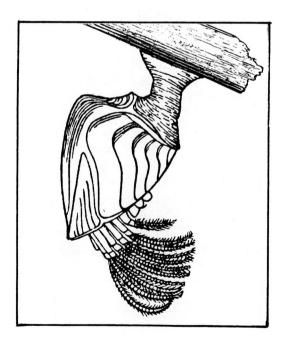

Goose Barnacle (LEPAS FASCICULARIS), *from an old German engraving, 1888.*

THE CARLINA

The carlina thistle *(Carlina vulgaris)* native to the Mediterranean region was an important magic love plant in medieval Europe. It was believed that its root gave a man the strength and sexual potency of a stallion. To get an effective carlina, you took topsoil from a rose garden in bloom, mixed it with sperma from a black stallion, planted a carlina in it at the stroke of midnight under a new moon, watered it with urine from a white mare and let it grow. It was then uprooted under the following new moon, cooked and eaten. Today the dried, highly hygroscopic carlina is used in rural parts of Europe as a weather-glass.

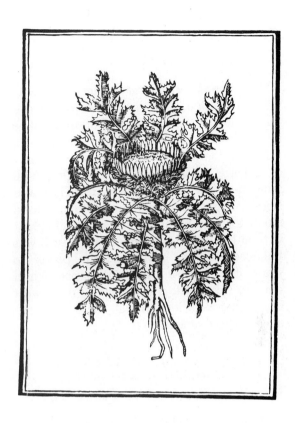

Carlina, Mattioli's COMMENTAIRES, *Lyons, 1579.*

THE DRAGON TREE

According to an ancient legend on the Solomon Islands, the first dragon tree *(Dracaena draco)* grew from the grave of the sea-monster *Pau Tangalu*. The tree itself, its leaves and its scale-covered cherry-sized fruits exuded a dark red resin called dragon's blood. In the South Sea Isles it was considered the most potent magic plant for all occasions. Dragon's blood, brought by Venetian merchants to Europe, was used in medieval times by deserted wives and maidens as an excellent love incense. If burned near an open window in their lonely bed-chambers for seven midnights in a row the escaping fumes would bring back the straying husband or lover sooner or later.

Dragon Tree, l'Ecluse's RARIORUM, *Antwerp, 1576.*

THE HONESTY

The honesty (*Lunaria annua*) native to
Central Europe, was also called Moonwort,
Silver-bloom or Satinpod. Its botanical name
is derived from the Latin *luna* — moon, in
reference to the shape and semi-transparency
of its large, oval seed pods, which glow with
a moon-silvery satin sheen. In the Dark and
Middle Ages sorcerers and witches used
moonwort as a highly important magic plant
in their brews and concoctions because it was
believed that the plant had the power to
ward off evil spirits, and put monsters and
demons to flight. Furthermore moonwort
could open door locks, break chains, and un-
shoe horses that trod on it.

Honesty, Gesner's RARIS HERBIS, *Zurich, 1555.*

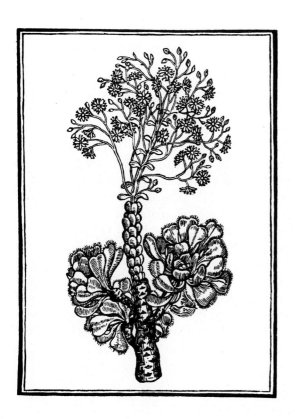

THE HOUSELEEK

The Old Dutch name of the houseleek
(*Sempervivum tectorum*) a rock plant, native
to Europe, was *Donderbloem* — thunder
flower. In the Dark Ages it was common belief that the plant gave the best protection
against lightning, fire, witches and evil
spirits. Charlemagne, King of the Franks,
first Emperor of the Holy Roman Empire
(768-814 A.D.) issued a law which made it
mandatory for every landlord to plant one
houseleek on the roof of his dwelling to protect it against fire, and to ward off war,
hunger and pestilence from the whole country. The houseleek became the symbol of
vivacity, because it retains its vivacious nature, even on the hot roof-tops.

Houseleek, l'Ecluse's RARIORUM, *Antwerp, 1576.*

THE ICE PLANT

The ice plant (*Mesembryanthemum crystallinum*) native to South Africa and the Mediterranean region is a member of the fig-marigold family. Its name is derived from its peculiar fleshy leaves which are covered with innumerable little, bladder-shaped, translucent vesicles filled with a limpid liquid. When the plant stands in the shade, it seems to be gemmed with dew drops; but when the ice plant is exposed to the burning sun, it appears to be scattered with tiny, frozen crystals which reflect with great brilliance the rays of the sun. The plant, which feels flaccid and cold to the touch, is considered to be the symbol of frigidity.

Ice Plant, from an old English Engraving.

THE MAIDENHAIR FERN

The maidenhair (*Adiantum capillus-veneris*), a fern with delicate fronds and slender stalks, was one of the magic plants of Roman mythology. It was believed to be the hair of Venus, goddess of love and beauty, who had risen from the foam of the sea. It is still called in French *cheveux de Venus* — hair of Venus. This belief was based on the wondrous quality of the maidenhair, which, when placed under water takes on a silvery magic sheen, and when removed is found to be perfectly dry, because water will not cling to it. In Roman symbolic magic, a potion made from powdered maidenhair fern was considered conducive in producing grace, beauty and love.

Maidenhair Fern, Mattioli's COMMENTAIRES, *1579.*

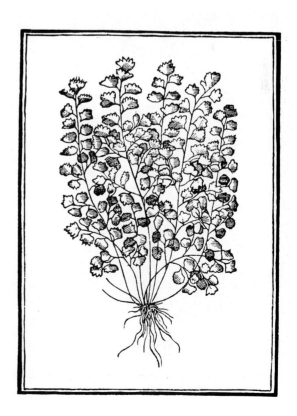

THE MANDRAKE

MANDRAKE, *from the* CODEX NEAPOLITANUS, *700 A.D. Vienna.*

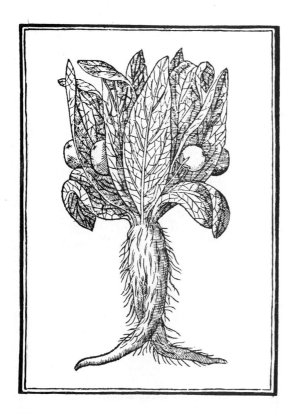

Masculine Mandragora (Mandrake), from Mattioli's
COMMENTAIRES, *Lyons, 1579.*

SPECIES MASCULI HUJUS HERBAE, *from Cuba's* HORTES
SANITATIS, *Paris, 1498.*

THE MANDRAKE

The mandrake *(Mandragora officinarum)*, a narcotic plant whose roots often grow in the shape of human limbs, is the oldest magic plant in botanical history. Already mentioned in the Bible as an ingredient for love-philtres *(Old Testament, Genesis XXX/14-15)*, it was called in Greek legend *Plant of Circe.* It was believed that Circe's magic brews, which turned men into swine, were infusions of the mandragora. In the Dark Ages its roots were an integral part of every witch's cauldron; and in the Middle Ages, a concoction of mandragora berries was used as an opiate and love-potion. It was common knowledge in medieval time that the mandrake grew under the gallows from the dripping semen of hanged men. Pulled from the ground the root emitted wild shrieks and those who heard them were driven mad. The safest way to secure a mandrake was to tie a dog to the plant on a moonless night. Plugging one's ears with beeswax and blowing a loud horn to drown out the shrieks, the dog was whipped at the stroke of midnight and the jumping animal pulled the screeching root from the ground and died. The English name of the plant, *mandrake*, means the dragon resembling man.

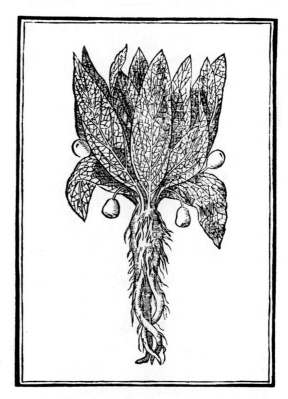

SPECIES FEMINAE HUJUS HERBAE, *from Cuba's* HORTUS SANITATIS, *Paris, 1498.*

Feminine Mandragora (Mandrake), from Mattioli's COMMENTAIRES, *Lyons, 1579.*

The Arbor Tristis, from Jacobus, NEUW KREÜTER-
BUCH, *Frankfort, 1613.*

THE TREE OF SORROW

The night-blooming tree of sorrow *(Arbor
tristis)* was believed to be a native South
American tree, whose trunk grew in the shape
of a female body. An ancient Amerindian
fable tells that the young and beautiful
daughter of the mighty chief and warrior,
Parizataco, fell in love with the sun. But when
the sun rejected her love and scorned her she
withdrew from all human companionship
into the wilderness. In her grief she slew herself. When her body was found by her people,
it was brought back to her native village and
put on a funeral pyre according to the custom
of her tribe and cremated. From the ashes of
her body sprang the Tree of Sorrow whose
beautiful blossoms never opened in daytime
in the presence of the sun. Its flowers un-
folded their petals only at night under the
cool light of the moon and the stars, filling
the night air with a fragrant, sweet-heavy
perfume. And when the sun rose in the morning the blossoms of this tree closed, its leaves
withered and the tree looked dead and barren, only to rejuvenate and unfold again
under the rays of the moon. Whenever a
human hand touched the blooming tree the
blossoms of this sensitive plant closed up and
their sweet scent vanished.

*Fanciful Picture of the Tree of Sorrow, from Dur-
ante's* HERBARIO NUOVO, *Rome, 1585.*

THE FLOWER CALENDAR

EVER SINCE MAN realized the eternal re-occurrence of Nature's cyclic behavior throughout the year, he tried to coordinate his sowing and gathering of food plants in accordance with this seasonal cycle. Seasons are man's arbitrary divisions of the year, characterized by the weather and the growth of vegetation. The term is derived from the Latin *serese* — to sow. The calendar of ancient Egypt had only three seasons: *Akhet* — the four months of sowing, *Pert* — the four months of growing, and *Shemu* — the four months of inundation. In the temperate zone of our lands we have four seasons in the calendar: winter, spring, summer and autumn. But in the semi-tropical regions of the globe there are still only three seasons: the dry, the rainy and the cold. In the equatorial tropics there are only two: the seasons of the torrid heat and of torrential rain. And along the Arctic circles there are also only two seasons: the long Arctic winter and the short Arctic summer.

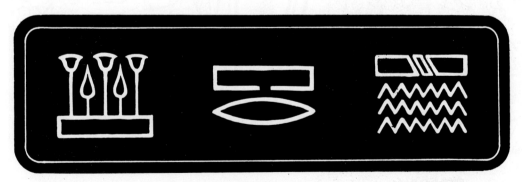

The Three Seasons of Ancient Egypt (Hieroglyphs), AKHET *— Winter,* PERT *— Spring, and* SHEMU *— Summer.*

THE SEASONS

Winter — the Season of Woodburning, from Le Rouge's GRANT KALENDRIER, *Troyes, 1496.*

THE SEASONS

Spring — the Season of Flowers, from Le Rouge's GRANT KALENDRIER, *Troyes, 1496.*

THE SEASONS

Summer — the Season of Harvest, from Le Rouge's GRANT KALENDRIER, *Troyes, 1496.*

THE SEASONS

Autumn — the Season of Vintage, from Le Rouge's GRANT KALENDRIER, *Troyes, 1496.*

THE SEASONS

Personification of Winter

Personification of Spring

Personification of Summer

Personification of Autumn

Personifications of the Four Seasons, from an English Broadside, 1682.

THE FLOWERS OF THE MONTHS

N THE CALENDARS of the Middle Ages the twelve divisional months of the year were always symbolized by the agricultural activities of the farmer, the chores of the farmer's wife, and by their few personal pleasures and relaxations. The calendar with its astronomical, meteorological and agronomical information was of the utmost importance to the farmer; more so than to persons of any other occupations. In the more easygoing and flirtatious 18th century and the literary and poetically inclined 19th century, the calendars of the Western World adopted the age-old Oriental custom of symbolizing the months through flowers and plants, according to their seasonal appearance.

The Twelve Months, from a Farmer's Calendar, Germany, 1493.

THE FLOWERS OF THE MONTHS

SNOWDROP — Flower of January

Flower of February — PRIMROSE

VIOLET — Flower of March

Flower of April — DAISY

HAWTHORN — Flower of May

Flower of June — HONEYSUCKLE

The Flowers of the Months, from an old English Calendar, 1866.

THE FLOWERS OF THE MONTHS

WATER LILY — Flower of July

Flower of August — POPPY

MORNING-GLORY — Flower of September

Flower of October — HOP

CHRYSANTHEMUM — Flower of November

Flower of December — HOLLY

The Flowers of the Months, from an old English Calendar, 1866.

THE CHINESE FLOWER CALENDAR

LOWERY LAND — HUA KUOH, as China is called is a land of beautiful gardens, designed to reproduce natural scenes as closely as possible, with grotesque rock formations, hills, streams, bamboo thickets, lotus and goldfish ponds, ornamental bridges, pavilions and wall openings, all so dear to the heart of the Chinese. Chinese gardens occupy only a small space in comparison with western gardens, with their extensive lawns and terraces, patterned parterres, and their geometrical flower beds and borders. It is considered vulgar to utilize for personal pleasure too much ground which should be used for raising crops, the most important business of life and survival. The extraordinary devotion to flowers has prevailed from early ages among the Chinese and symbolic meaning was assigned to every flower since antiquity. The Chinese even have a special deity of flowers. According to legend, Ho Hsien-ku, daughter of a humble shopkeeper in Lingling, Hunan, who lived in the 7th century, A.D. ate

CANOPUS, *God of Longevity Issuing from a Peach. Old Chinese Engraving.*

HO-HSIEN-KU, *Taoist Genius of Flowers. Old Chinese Engraving.*

THE CHINESE FLOWER CALENDAR

from a peach of immortality given to her by Canopus, god of longevity. She became the genius of flowers, one of the eight Taoist immortals. She decreed that reverence should be paid to a special flower for each month of the calendar year; this Chinese Flower Calendar, the oldest of its kind, was copied throughout the centuries in the Orient and Occident.

China the Flowery Land, from an old Chinese Engraving.

THE CHINESE FLOWER CALENDAR

PLUM BLOSSOM – MEI HUA
Flower of January and Winter
Symbol of Beauty and Longevity

TAO HUA – PEACH BLOSSOM
Flower of February
Symbol of Longevity and Marriage

TREE PEONY – MU TAN
Flower of March and Spring
Symbol of Love and Affection

YING HÚA – CHERRY BLOSSOM
Flower of April
Emblem of the Feminine Principle

MAGNOLIA – MU LAN
Flower of May
Symbol of Feminine Sweetness

TAN TSAO – POMEGRANATE
Flower of June
Symbol of Progeny and Posterity

THE CHINESE FLOWER CALENDAR

LOTUS FLOWER – LIEN HUA
Flower of July and Summer
Symbol of Perfection and Purity

LI HUA – PEAR BLOSSOM
Flower of August
Symbol of Purity and Longevity

MALLOW BLOSSOM – KUAI HUA
Flower of September
Magic Charm against Evil Spirits

CHU HUA – CHRYSANTHEMUM
Flower of October and Autumn
Symbol of Harvest, Rest and Ease

GARDENIA – PAI CH'AN
Flower of November

A FU JUNG – POPPY
Flower of December
Emblem of Evil and Dissipation

THE JAPANESE FLOWER CALENDAR

The Japanese, like the Chinese, are one of the most flower conscious people of the world. Not only is their culture and literature rich in flower lore and legend, but they also developed the more than 1,000 year old symbolic flower art of *Hana-ike* (flower arrangement), or *Ikebana* (arranged flowers). So deep is the attachment to flowers in the Japanese that even the oldest

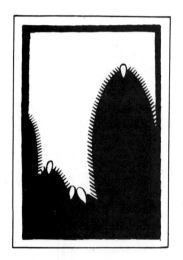

Pine — Matsu
Flower of January

Plum — Ume
Flower of February

Cherry — Sakura
Flower of March

Wisteria — Fuji
Flower of April

Iris — Ayame
Flower of May

Peony — Botan
Flower of June

Flowers of the Months, from HANA-AWASE, *the Flower Matching Game.*

THE JAPANESE FLOWER CALENDAR

and most popular card game in Japan, *Hana-garuta*, a sort of bridge-poker, played with 48 cards, has twelve suits representing the symbolic Japanese Flowers of the Months. Only the month of August has no flower emblem: its symbol is the Hill Crest over which the August Moon, emblem of good fortune, rises.

Mountain Clover — Hagi
Flower of July

Hill Crest — Oka
Symbol of August

Chrysanthemum — Kiku
Flower of September

Maple — Momiji
Flower of October

Willow — Yanagi
Flower of November

Paulownia — Kiri
Flower of December

Flowers of the Months, from HANA-AWASE, *the Flower Matching Game.*

THE JAPANESE FLOWER CALENDAR

AKI-NO-NANA-KUSA, *the Seven Flowers of Autumn.*

The Seven Herbs of Autumn, already mentioned in *Manyoshu,* the 8th century *Collection of a Myriad Leaves,* are an important part of the Japanese Flower Calendar. These seven herbs are: Bellflower, Bush Clover, Eulalia, Kuzu Vine, Pink, Patrinia, and Thoroughwort.

THE LANGUAGE of FLOWERS

SENTIMENTS AND SYMBOLISM

URING THE EASYGOING time of bygone days when chivalry was still alive, flirtation and courtesy a part of daily living, flowers and poems were the only gifts exchanged by lovers. Since antiquity, mythology and religion, folklore and legend, magic and superstitious belief assigned to flowers certain emblematic symbolism. Every bouquet and garland, nosegay and posy, corsage and boutonniere, festoon and wreath was carefully composed according to its legendary meaning. Joy and grief, triumph and woe, admiration and gratitude, love and desire, every human sentiment had its floral emblem. *Selam*, the Oriental Language of Flowers was an old Persian poetical art introduced into Europe by Charles II, king of Sweden, who, after his defeat at Poltava in 1709 by Peter the Great, czar of Russia, fled into exile to Turkey. He lived for 5 years at the Ottomanian court, and returned in 1714 to Sweden, from where his courtiers started the mode of the Flower Language throughout the Western World. There was no more important language for the 18th and 19th century beaux and belles than the Language of Flowers. *Durch die Blume sprechen — Speaking through Flowers* became a Western proverb, meaning any flowery or poetic expression with a hidden significance or a message of love.

109

ROEMIO DI SER ALEXANDRO BRACCIO al preftantiffimo & excellen tiffimo giouene Lorenzo Pierfrancefco de medici fopra la traductione duna hiftoria di due amã ti compofta dalla felice memoria di papa pio fecódo.

The Lovers, from Piccolomini's (Pope Pius II) HISTORIA DI DUE AMATI, *Milan, 1510.*

SENTIMENTS AND SYMBOLISM

Absinth, or **Wormwood**
Separation and Torment of Love
Bitterness and Heartache
Herb of Mars (*Astrological*).

Acacia Blossom
Beauty in Retirement and Platonic Love
Bad Luck Gift to a Woman

Acanthus Leaves
Admiration of the Arts

Aconite, or **Monkshood**
Misanthropy and Poisonous Words
Symbol of Crime
Herb of Saturn (*Astrological*)

Acorn
Symbol of Life and Immortality (*Nordic*)

Adam's Needle
A Friend in Need

Adonis
Recollection of Life's Pleasure
Flower of New Year's Eve (*Japanese*)
Symbol of Gold and Wealth (*Japanese*)
Fortune-Longevity Plant (*Japanese*)

Agave
Tree of Life and Abundance (*Mexican*)

Alder Tree, or **Elm Tree**
Genesis Tree of Embla, the Woman (*Nordic*)
Tree of the Fairies (*Celtic*)
Tree of Divination (*Old Irish*)

Almond
Virginity and Fruitfulness
Symbol of Happy Marriage (*French*)

Almond Blossom
Hope and Watchfulness
Flower of the Annunciation

Almond Tree
Tree of Heaven (*Persian*)
Tree of January (*Semitic*)

Almond Twins
Lover's Charm and Symbol of Good Luck

Aloe
Wisdom and Integrity
Dedicated to Zeus and Jupiter

Amaranth
Constancy and Fidelity
Faith and Immortality
"My love will never fade or die!"

Amaryllis
Pastoral Poetry

Anemone
Refusal and Abandonment
"Go away!"
Dedicated to Aphrodite and Venus

Apple
Symbol of Perpetual Concord
Dedicated to Aphrodite and Venus
"Peace be with you!" (*Chinese*)
Good Luck Gift

Apricot Blossom
Timid Love
Emblem of the Fair Sex (*Chinese*)

Arbor Infelix
Tree of Crucifixion

Arbor Vitae, or **Thuya Tree**
Tree of Life
Unchanging Friendship

Artemisia Leaf
Symbol of Dignity (*Chinese*)

Ash Tree
Tree of Life (*Nordic*)
Genesis Tree of Ask, the Man (*Nordic*)

Aspen, or **Trembling Poplar**
Lamentation and Fear

Asphodel
Languor and Regret
Symbol of Death (*Greek*)

Aster
Elegance and Daintiness
Talisman of Love
Herb of Venus (*Astrological*)

Autumn Bell, or **Fringed Gentian**
Flower emblem of Autumn (*Occidental*)

Wreath of Laurel, Victory Symbol, by Aldus Manutius, Venice, 1499.

Azalea
Fragile and Ephemeral Passion
Emblem of Womanhood *(Chinese)*

Balm, or **Melissa**
Sympathy and Love
Symbol of Rejuvenation *(Arabic)*

Bamboo
Friend of China
Symbol of Graceful Strength *(Chinese)*
Durability and Longevity *(Chinese)*
Candidness and Devotion *(Japanese)*

Bamboo Staff
Mourning for a Father *(Chinese)*

Banana Tree
Birth and Life Tree of the Tropics

Barrel of Fruit, or **Vegetables**
Symbol of Abundance

Bay Tree
Glory and Resurrection *(Roman)*

Bean
Immortality and Transmigration
Magic and Mysticism

Beech Tree
Oracle and Divination *(Greek)*
Dedicated to Zeus and Jupiter
Prosperity and Pleasant Memory
Flower Emblem of Denmark

Begonia
"Beware! I am fanciful!"

Belladonna
"I bring you bad luck!"
Fatal Gift to a Man

*Crown of Roses, Superior Merit, by William Cop-
land, London, 1548.*

Bindweed
Coquette and Busybody
Passing Attachment without Consequence

Birch Tree
Light and Fertility
Dedicated to Thor and Donar
Flower Emblem of Estonia

Blackthorn, or **Sloe**
Difficulty and Austerity
"There are many obstacles to our love!"
Bad Luck Gift to a Woman

Bluebell, or **Harebell**
Delicacy and Humility
Emblem of St. George

Bo Tree, or **Pipal Tree**
Meditation and Perfection
Tree of Nirvana *(Buddhist)*
Dedicated to Gautama Buddha

Borage
Symbol of Courage *(Medieval)*

Bouquet of Full-blown Roses
Token of Gratitude

Bouquet of Withered Flowers
Token of Rejected Love

Box Tree
Firmness and Stoicism in Adversity
"I never change!"

Box Holly, or **Butcher's Broom**
Activity and Cleanliness

Brake, or **Eagle Fern**
Confidence and Shelter

Bramble
Envy and Jealousy
Bad Luck Gift to a Woman

Brier
Solitude and Thoughtfulness
Courage and Strength
Herb of Mars *(Astrological)*
Bad Luck Gift to a Woman

Broom Plant, or **Planta Genista**
Ardor and Humility
Badge of the Plantagenet Kings of England
Flower Emblem of Brittany

Buckeye, or **Horse Chestnut**
Luxury and Health
Good Luck Charm for a Man

Buddha's Hand, or **Citrus Medica**
Blessings of Buddha *(Chinese)*

Bundle of Birch Rods, or **Fasces**
Union and Strength
Symbol of Lictorian Authority *(Roman)*

Burdock
Importunity and Boredom
"Do not touch me!"

Buttercup
Mockery and Sarcasm
Ingratitude and Spite
Dedicated to Mars and Ares

Cactus
Bravery and Endurance (*Amerindian*)
Fairy's Hand (*Chinese*)
Bad Luck to a Pregnant Woman (*Chinese*)

Camellia
Excellence and Steadfastness
"I shall love you always!"
Good Luck Gift to a Man
Symbol of Sudden Death (*Japanese*)

Camomile
Initiative and Ingenuity
Energy in Adversity
Herb of Mercury (*Astrological*)

Canterbury Bell
Constancy and Warning
Emblem of St. Thomas

Cardinal Flower
Distinction and Splendor

Carnation, Pink
Flower Emblem of Mother's Day

Carnation, Purple
Antipathy and Capriciousness

Carnation, Red
Admiration and Worldly Sentiments

Carnation, White
Pure and Ardent Love
Good Luck Gift to a Woman

Carnation, Yellow
Distain and Rejection

Cassia Tree
World Tree and Tree of Life (*Chinese*)

Cattail
Peace and Prosperity (*Amerindian*)

Cedar Tree
Nobility and Incorruptibility
Flower Emblem of Lebanon

Cherry Blossom
Symbol of Good Education (*Chinese*)
Flower of April (*Chinese*)
Wealth and Prosperity (*Japanese*)
Flower of March (*Japanese*)
National Flower of Japan

Cherry Twins
Good Luck Symbol and Lover's Charm

Cherry-apple Blossom
Emblem of Feminine Beauty (*Chinese*)
Symbol of Peace and Concord (*Chinese*)

Chestnut
Independence and Injustice
Bad Luck Gift to a Woman

China Aster
Jealousy and After-thought

"I shall fight against fate!" (*Selam*)

Chrysanthemum
Cheerfulness and Optimism
Flower of November (*Occidental*)
Rest and Ease (*Chinese*)
Flower of October (*Chinese*)
Badge of the Old Chinese Army
Long Life and Happiness (*Japanese*)
Flower of September (*Japanese*)
Kikumon — Imperial Crest of Japan

Cinnamon
Love and Beauty
"My fortune is yours!" (*Selam*)
Dedicated to Aphrodite and Venus

Clematis
Artifice and Ingenuity
Good Luck Gift to a Woman

Clove
Dignity and Restraint
"I love you secretly!" (*Selam*)

Clover
Fertility and Domestic Virtue
Symbol of Trinity
Good Luck Gift to a Woman

Clover, Five-leaved
Symbol of Bad Luck

Clover, Four-leaved
Symbol of Good Luck

Cockscomb, or **Celosia**
Silliness and Foppery

Coconut Palm
Tropical Tree of Life and Abundance

Wreath of Flowers, Flora's Diadem, by Federix de Vinciolo, Paris, 1606.

Coltsfoot
Maternal Love and Care

Columbine
Cuckoldry and Deserted Lover
Fool's Staff Flower
Bad Luck Gift to a Man

Convolvulus
Humble Perseverance
Good Luck Gift to a Woman
Love and Marriage (*Chinese*)

Coriander
"You have hidden merits!" (*Selam*)

Corn Cockle
Inocent Charm and Daintiness
Good Luck Gift to a Woman

Cornucopia, or **Horn of Plenty**
Horn of the Goat Althea (*Greek*)
Symbol of Abundance

Crane's-bill, or **Wild Geranium**
Constancy and Availability
"I desire to please!"

Crocus
Youthful Gladness and Attachment

Crown Imperial
Majesty and Power

Crown of Laurel
Symbol of Victory at the Pythian Games
Dedicated to Apollo (*Greek*)

Crown of Parsley
Symbol of Victory at the Nemean Games
Dedicated to Zeus (*Greek*)

Crown of Pine
Symbol of Victory at the Isthmian Games
Dedicated to Poseidon (*Greek*)

Crown of Roses
Symbol of Superior Merit

Crown of Thorns
Symbol of Martyrdom (*Biblical*)

Crown of Wild Olives
Symbol of Victory at the Olympian Games
Dedicated to Zeus (*Greek*)

Currant
"I am worthy of you!" (*Selam*)

Cyclamen
Resignation and Good-bye
Bad Luck Gift to a Woman

Cypress Tree
Mourning and Lament (*Occidental*)
Symbol of Death (*Greek*)
Emblem of Grace and Joy (*Oriental*)

Daffodil
Emblem of the Annunciation
Flower of Easter

Dahlia
Treachery and Instability
Sterility and Misrepresentation
"Many words but no soul!"

Daisy
Gentleness and Innocence
Purity in Thought and Loyal Love
Flower of April (*Occidental*)
Dedicated to Aphrodite and Venus
Good Luck Gift to a Woman

Damask Rose
Ambassador of Love (*Persian*)

Dandelion
Oracle of Time and Love
"Faithful to you!"

Cornucopia of Flowers, by Christoffel van Sichem II, Amsterdam, 1646.

Date Palm
Tree of the Calendar Year *(Egyptian)*
Sacred Emblem of Judea
Tree of Life and Abundance *(Arabic)*
Symbol of Fecundity *(Chinese)*

Datura, or **Thorn Apple**
Deceitful Charm
"You are poison!"
Devil's Herb *(Gypsy Lore)*

Day Lily, or **Hemerocallis**
Emblem of the Mother *(Chinese)*

Dead Leaves
Sadness and Melancholy
Symbol of Autumn *(Occidental)*

Digitalis, or **Foxglove**
Treacherous Magnificence
"You are beautiful but careless!"

Dipsacus, or **Teasel**
Flower which keeps the Dew
"I thirst after you!"

Dog Grass
War and Death
Dedicated to Mars *(Roman)*

Dog Rose
Love and Poetry
Hope and Fear
"You have enchanted me!"

Dogwood
Love in Adversity

Dried Figs, or **Dried Prunes**
Emaciation and Sterility
Bad Luck Gift to a Woman

Edelweiss
Daring and Noble Courage
Purity and Immortality
Emblem of Alpine Achievement
National Flower of Switzerland

Eglantine
Spring and Poetry

Elderberry Blossom
Humility and Kindness
Compassion and Zeal

Elecampane, or **Helenium**
Woe and Tears
"You are hurting me!" *(Selam)*
Flower of Helen of Troy *(Greek)*

Everlasting Flower
Attachment and Constancy
"Always yours!"
Good Luck Gift to a Woman

Everlasting Pea
Sweet and Constant Memory

Evening Primula
Inconstancy and Fickleness

Festoon of Laurel
Emblem of Victory

Fig Tree
Peace and Abundance *(Hebrew)*
Tree of Heaven *(Arabic)*
Wisdom and Integrity
Tree of Jupiter *(Astrological)*

Filix-mas, or **Male Fern**
Confidence and Fascination
Good Luck Gift to a Woman
The Lucky Hands *(Mongolian)*
Occultism and Power *(Mongolian)*
Talisman of Genghis Khan

Fir Tree
Boldness and Fidelity
Dedicated to Pan *(Greek)*

Basket of Vegetables, by Christoffel van Sichem II, Amsterdam, 1646.

Basket of Flowers, from Stalker's TREATISE OF JAPANING, *Oxford, 1688.*

Integrity and Ingenuity
Tree of Mercury *(Astrological)*
Lasting Affection and Eternity *(Chinese)*
Good Luck Gift to Departing Friends *(Chinese)*

Fleur-de-lis
Flame of Light, Life and Power
National Emblem of France

Forget-me-not, or **Myosotis**
Faithful Love and Undying Memory
Good Luck Gift to a Woman

Fuchsia
Amiability, Anxiety and Confiding Love

Fungus, or **Ling Chih**
Divine Plant of China
Symbol of Everlasting Life *(Taoist)*

Furze, or **Gorse**
Cheerfulness in Adversity
"My thoughts for you are like golden
butterflies!"
Good Luck Gift to a Woman

Garden Balsam, or **Impatiens**
Refusal and Severed Ties
"Touch me not, you have offended me!"

Gardenia
"I love you in secret!"
Good Luck Gift to a Man
Flower of November *(Chinese)*

Garland of Flowers
Love's Bondage

Garlic
Courage and Strength
Herb of Mars *(Astrological)*

Geranium
Folly and Stupidity
"You are childish!"
Bad Luck Gift to a Man

Ginseng
Strength and Longevity *(Chinese)*
Clear Judgment and Vigor *(Chinese)*

Gladiolus, or **Sword Lily**
Flower of the Gladiators *(Roman)*
"You pierce my heart!"

Globe Flower, or **Luckan Gowan**
Witches' Gold *(Scottish)*

Goldenrod, or **Solidago**
Treasure and Good Fortune

Grapes
Token of Canaan, the Promised Land
Peace and Abundance *(Biblical)*
Symbol of the Wine of the Eucharist
Good Luck Gift

Grass
Utility and Submission
Bad Luck Gift to a Woman

Bouquet of Flowers, from Stalker's TREATISE OF JAPANING, *Oxford, 1688.*

Green Leaves
  Revived Hope
Guelder Rose
  Whitsuntide Flower (*English*)
Hawthorn
  Sweet Hope and Marriage
  "You are my only queen!"
  Dedicated to Hymen (*Greek*)
  Flower of May (*Occidental*)
  Good Luck Gift to a Woman
Hazelnut Tree
  Communication, Reconciliation and Peace
  Dedicated to Mercury (*Greek*)
  Tree of Wisdom (*Celtic*)
  Tree of Thor and Donar (*Nordic*)
  Emblem of St. Philibert
Heartsease
  Happiness in Recollection
Heather, Purple
  Beauty in Solitude and Admiration
Heather, White
  Protection from Danger (*Scottish*)
  "Your wish will come true!"

*The Carnation, Symbol of Mother-Love, Silhouette
by P. O. Runge, Germany, 1800.*

Heliotrope
  Eternal Love and Devoted Attachment
  Dedicated to Apollo (*Greek*)
  Herb of the Sun (*Astrological*)
Hellebore
  Madness and Delirium (*Medieval*)
Hemlock
  Perfidy and Death
  Poison-cup of Socrates (*Greek*)
  "We who must die!"
  Bad Luck Gift
Hepatica, or Liverwort
  Confidence and Cure
Hibiscus
  Delicate Beauty
Honesty, or Satinflower
  Money in all Pockets
Holly
  Foresight and Defence
  "I dare not approach!"
  Flower of December (*Occidental*)
Hollyhock
  Ambition and Liberality
  Symbol of Nature and Fecundity (*Chinese*)
Honeysuckle
  Devotion and Affection
  Generosity and Gaiety
  Bond of Love
  "We belong to each other!" (*Selam*)
  Flower of June (*Occidental*)
Hop Plant
  Injustice and Destruction
  "I overcome all difficulties!" (*Selam*)
  Flower of October (*Occidental*)
Horse-radish
  Bitter Herb of Bondage (*Jewish Passover*)
Houseleek
  Symbol of Vivacity
  "My friendship for life!"
Hyacinth
  Games and Sport
  Rashness and Woe (*Greek*)
  Dedicated to Apollo (*Greek*)
Hydrangea
  Boastfulness and Frigidity
  "Beautiful without scent and fruit!"
  Bad Luck Gift to a Woman
Ice Plant
  Frigidity and Heartlessness
  "Your looks freeze me!"
Iris
  Faith, Wisdom and Valor
  Hope, Light and Power
  Eloquence, Message and Promise
  Flower Emblem of France (*Fleur-de-lis*)
  Dedicated to the Virgin Mary

Herb of the Moon (*Astrological*)
Good Luck Gift to a Man
Emblem of the Warrior (*Japanese*)
Flower of May (*Japanese*)

Ivy
Attachment and Eternal Friendship
Fidelity and Wedded Love
"I die where I cling!"
Dedicated to Dionysus and Bacchus

Jack-in-the-Pulpit
Ardor and Zeal

Jasmine, Red
Folly and Glee
"Our love will be intoxicating!" (*Selam*)

Jasmine, White
Amiability and Cheerfulness
"Our love will be sweet!" (*Selam*)
Symbol of Womanly Sweetness (*Chinese*)

Jasmine, Yellow
Timidity and Modesty
"Our love will be passionate!" (*Selam*)
Flower of Epiphany

Job's Tears
Repentance and Faith

Jonquil
Violent Sympathy and Desire
"Have pity on my passion!" (*Selam*)

Juniper
Confidence and Protection
Initiative and Ingenuity
Herb of Mercury (*Astrological*)

Laburnum
Refusal and Loneliness
"You have broken my heart!"

Lady's Slipper
Capricious Beauty

Larkspur
Open Heart and Ardent Attachment

Laurel
Success and Renown
Glory and Victory
"I shall conquer you!"
Dedicated to Apollo (*Greek*)
Luck and Pride
Plant of the Sun (*Astrological*)

Lavender
Constancy and Loyalty
Sweetness and Undying Love
"Fervent but silent love!"
Good Luck Gift to a Woman
Herb of Mercury (*Astrological*)

Leek
Flower Emblem of Wales
Dedicated to St. David

Lemon
Symbol of Harvest (*Jewish Succoth*)

Lemon Tree
Passion and Discretion
Luck and Pride
Tree of the Sun (*Astrological*)

Lilac, Mauve
"Do you still love me?" (*Selam*)

Lilac, Pink
Youth and Acceptance (*Occidental*)
Good Luck Gift to a Woman
Friction and Strife (*Chinese*)

Lilac, White
"My first dream of love!" (*Selam*)

Lily, Orange
Hatred and Disdain

Lily, White
Sincerity and Majesty
Purity and Virginity
Symbol of Motherhood (*Semitic*)
Dedicated to Hèra and Juno
Easter Flower
Emblem of the Virgin Mary
Rod of St. Joseph
Good Luck Gift to a Woman

The Rose, Symbol of Love, Silhouette, Austria, 1800.

Lily-of-the-Valley
Purity and Humility
Tears of the Virgin Mary
Sweetness and Renewed Happiness
"Let us make up!"
Flower of Spring
Whitsuntide Flower *(English)*

Linden Tree
Conjugal Love and Marital Virtues
Tree of Baucis *(Greek)*

Locust Tree, or **Robinia**
Affection beyond the Grave

Lotus
Mystery and Truth
Symbol of the Sun *(Persian)*
Creation and Resurrection *(Egyptian)*
Flower Emblem of Egypt
Golden Throne of Brahma *(Hindu)*
National Flower of India
Symbol of Heaven *(Buddhist)*
Fruitfulness and Offspring *(Chinese)*
Perfection and Purity *(Chinese)*
Flower of July *(Chinese)*
Emblem of Summer *(Chinese)*
Past, Present and Future *(Japanese)*
Flower of Midsummer *(Japanese)*

Love-in-a-Mist, or **Nigella**
Delicacy and Perplexity
"Butterfly wings of our love!"
Dedicated to St. Catherine

Love-lies-Bleeding
"Hopeless not heartless!"

Basket of Flowers, Valentine, Silhouette, Germany, 1820.

Madonna Lily
Resurrection and Annunciation
Flower of Easter
Dedicated to the Virgin Mary

Magnolia
Splendid Beauty and Sweetness
Flower of May *(Chinese)*

Maidenhair Fern
Secret Bond of Love
Dedicated to Aphrodite and Venus

Mallow
Delicate Beauty and Gentle Affection
Maternal Tenderness and Beneficence
Flower of September *(Chinese)*

Mandrake, or **Mandragora**
Conception and Fruitfulness *(Biblical)*
Plant of Circe *(Greek)*
Devil's Candle *(Arabic)*
Root of Black Magic *(Medieval)*

Maple Leaves
Symbol of Autumn *(Occidental)*
Flower Emblem of Canada
Lover's Valentine *(Japanese)*
Flower of October *(Japanese)*

Maple Tree
Reserve and Retirement

Marigold
Disquietude and Jealousy
Grief and Sorrow
"What is the matter with you?"

Marjoram
Comfort and Consolation
Kindness and Courtesy
Mascot Flower for Lovers *(Gypsy Lore)*

Bouquet of Flowers, Valentine, Silhouette, Germany, 1800.

Heart of Branches, Valentine, Silhouette, England, 1820.

Marsh Marigold
Pensiveness and Winning Grace
"You are my divinity!"

Marvel-of-Peru
Flame of Love

Meadow Saffron
"Our pleasant days are over!"
"Let us separate!"
Flower of Autumn (*Occidental*)
Bad Luck Gift to a Woman

Mecca Balsam
Balm of Gilead (*Biblical*)
Improvement and Cure (*Turkish*)

Medlar
Timidity and Peevishness
Bad Luck Gift to a Man

Mignonette
Modesty and Hidden Beauty
"Your qualities surpass your charm!"

Milfoil, or Yarrow
Disputes and Quarrels
Emblem of War (*Greek*)
Herb of Achilles (*Greek*)

Mimosa
Daintiness and sensibility
"Be careful, do not hurt me!"

Mint
Violent Love and Consolation
Plant of Jupiter (*Astrological*)

Mistletoe
Affection and Love
"I shall surmount all difficulties."
Good Luck Gift to a Woman
Magic Plant of the Druids (*Celtic*)

Sacred Plant of India

Molucca Bean, or Virgin Mary's Nut
Good Luck Charm (*English*)

Morning Glory
Farewell and Departure
Flower of September (*Occidental*)
Symbol of Mortality (*Japanese*)

Moss
"Charity, nothing more!"
Bad Luck Gift to a Woman

Moss Rose
Superiority and Pleasure

Mountain Ash, or Rowan Tree
Antidote and Mercy
Tree against Magic and Sorcery (*Nordic*)
Dedicated to Thor and Donar (*Nordic*)

Mountain Clover
Fecundity, Conquest and Victory (*Japanese*)
Flower of July (*Japanese*)

Mulberry Staff
Mourning for a Mother (*Chinese*)

Mulberry Tree, Red
Symbol of Unhappy Love
"I shall not survive you!" (*Selam*)
Tree of Pyramus and Thisbe (*Babylonian*)
Tree of Sorrow (*Chinese*)

Mulberry Tree, White
Wisdom and Immortality
Industry and Comfort of Home (*Chinese*)

Mullein
Herb of Love (*Medieval*)

Bouquet of Flowers, Valentine, Silhouette, Vienna, 1820.

Mushroom
Wisdom and Integrity
Plant of Jupiter *(Astrological)*

Musk Rose
Capricious Beauty

Myrtle
Love, Mirth and Joy *(Egyptian)*
Flower of Hathor *(Egyptian)*
Emblem of Marriage *(Hebrew)*
Flower of the Tabernacle *(Hebrew)*
Dedicated to Aphrodite and Venus

Nandina
Sacred and Heavenly Bamboo *(Japanese)*
Symbol of Clear Air *(Japanese)*
Gift of Purification *(Japanese)*

Narcissus
Egotism and Conceit
Plant of Nemesis *(Greek)*
Symbol of Good Fortune *(Chinese)*
Emblem of Winter *(Chinese)*
Mirth and Joyousness *(Japanese)*
Emblem of Formality *(Japanese)*

Nasturtium, or Tropaeolum
Conquest and Victory in Battle

Nettle
Cruelty and Slander
"You break my heart!"
Bad Luck Gift to a Woman

Nuts
"You are cracked!"
Bad Luck Gift to a Man

Oak Leaf Cluster
Token of Heroism and Victory *(Teutonic)*

Wreath of Flowers, Flora's Diadem, by Gustav Bethge, Berlin, 1838.

Oak Tree
Stability and Hospitality
Tree of Philemon *(Greek)*
Dedicated to Zeus and Jupiter
Tree of Life *(Nordic)*
Dedicated to Thor and Donar
Celestial Tree of the Druids *(Celtic)*
Symbol of Masculine Strength *(Chinese)*

Oleander
Beauty and Grace *(Chinese)*

Olive Branch
Safe Travel *(Biblical)*
Peace and Reconciliation
Emblem of the Archangel Gabriel

Olive Tree
Fidelity and Fruitfulness
Dedicated to Athene and Minerva
Emblem of Studious Pursuit *(Chinese)*

Orange
Happiness and Prosperity *(Chinese)*
New Year's Goodwill Gift *(Chinese)*

Orange Blossom
Virginity and Innocence
"I shall not sin!" *(Selam)*
Marriage and Fruitfulness *(Saracen)*
Chastity and Eternal Love *(Japanese)*

Orange Tree
Generosity and Fecundity

Orchid
Flower of Magnificence
"I await your favors!" *(Selam)*
Symbol of Love and Beauty *(Chinese)*
Refinement and Fragrance *(Chinese)*
Symbol of Numerous Progeny *(Confucian)*

Our Lady's Bedstraw
Symbol of the Nativity

Ox-Eye Daisy
Flower of Midsummer Day
Dedicated to St. John the Baptist

Palm Leaves
Victory and Conquest
Success and Peace
Symbol of Harvest *(Hebrew Succoth)*
Symbol of Martyrdom *(Catacombs)*
Emblem of Palm Sunday
Dignity and Felicity *(Chinese)*
Emblem of Retirement *(Chinese)*

Palm Tree
Creative Power and Peace *(Semitic)*
Flower Emblem of Judea

Pansy
Thoughtful Recollection
Flower Emblem of Trinity Sunday
Good Luck Gift to a Man

Parma Violet
"Let me love you!"

Pasqueflower
Flower Emblem of Easter

Passionflower
Faith and Piety
Symbol of the Passion *(Spanish)*

Paulownia
Justice and Benevolence *(Japanese)*
Flower of December *(Japanese)*
Kirimon — Crest of the Empress of Japan

Pea
Happy Marriage and Fertility

Peach
Fruit of Eternal Life *(Chinese)*
Good Luck Gift to a Man

Peach Blossom
Bridal Hope and Generosity *(Chinese)*
Flower of February *(Chinese)*
Feminine Softness and Matrimony *(Japanese)*
Emblem of Springtime *(Japanese)*

Peach Stones
Good Luck Charm for Children *(Chinese)*

Peach Tree
Tree of the Fairy Fruit *(Chinese)*
Emblem of Immortality *(Japanese)*

Pear
Badge of Actors and Musicians *(Chinese)*

Pear Blossom
Health and Hope
Purity and Longevity *(Chinese)*
Flower of August *(Chinese)*

Pear Tree
Wise Justice and Good Government *(Chinese)*

Peony
Plant of Healing *(Greek)*
Gay Life and Prosperity *(Japanese)*
Happy Marriage and Virility *(Japanese)*
Flower of June *(Japanese)*

Periwinkle
Sweet Memories and Unerring Devotion

Persea Tree
Symbol of Fame *(Egyptian)*

Persimmon
Symbol of Joy *(Chinese)*
Emblem of Victory *(Japanese)*

Petunia
Anger and Resentment
"I am furious!"

Philodendron
The Loving Tree

Phlox
Sweet Dreams and Proposal of Love

Pine Cone
Life and Fecundity *(Semitic)*

Pine Needle Twins
Faithfulness and Conjugal Love *(Japanese)*

Pine Tree
Boldness and Fidelity
Dedicated to Poseidon and Neptune
Symbol of Friendship *(Chinese)*
Stability and Strong Old Age *(Japanese)*
Flower of January *(Japanese)*

Pink, Red
Ardent Love and Pure Affection

Pink, White
Refusal and Departure

Pink, Yellow
Disdain and Rejection

Plane Tree
Genius and Magnificence *(Persian)*

Plantain
Symbol of Self Education *(Chinese)*

Plum Blossom
"Keep your promises!" *(Selam)*
Beauty and Longevity *(Chinese)*
Flower of January *(Chinese)*
Emblem of Winter *(Chinese)*
Happiness and Marriage *(Japanese)*
Flower of February *(Japanese)*
Emblem of Spring *(Japanese)*

Plum Tree
Taoist Tree of Longevity *(Chinese)*
Patience and Perseverance *(Japanese)*
Emblem of the Samurai *(Japanese)*

Poinsettia
Christmas Flower *(North American)*

Pomegranate
Life and Fecundity *(Semitic)*
Dedicated to Hera and Juno

*Wreath of Flowers, Flora's Diadem, by Lotte Jäger,
Tuebingen, 1853.*

Symbol of a Hopeful Future *(Oriental)*
Good Luck Gift to a Woman
Flower Emblem of Granada — Spain
Badge of Catherine of Aragon

Pomegranate Blossom
Symbol of Posterity *(Chinese)*
Flower of June *(Chinese)*

Poppy
Eternal Sleep and Oblivion *(Greek)*
Dedicated to all Nocturnal Deities
Flower of August *(Occidental)*
Emblem of Memorial Day
Flower of December *(Chinese)*
Imagination and Dreaminess
Herb of the Moon *(Astrological)*

Primrose
Early Youth and Young Love
Flower of February *(Occidental)*

Pussy Willow
Flower Symbol of Easter

Ragged Robin
Curiosity and Dandyism

Ragwort
"I am humble but proud!"

Reed
Symbol of Music
Plant of Pan *(Greek)*

Rocket
Lust and Vanity
Dedicated to Priapus *(Greek)*

Rohdea
Green for Ten Thousand Years *(Japanese)*

Symbol of Happy Retirement *(Japanese)*

Rose, Full-blown
"I love you" *(Selam)*

Rose, Pink
"Our love is perfect happiness!" *(Selam)*

Rose, Red
Love and Desire
"May you be pleased and your sorrows mine!"
(Selam)
Dedicated to Aphrodite and Venus
Flower of Eros and Cupid
Emblem of the Martyrs
Good Luck Gift to a Woman
Badge of the House of Lancaster

Rose, White
Charm and Innocence
"You are so pure and lovely!" *(Selam)*
Emblem of Harpocrates *(Greek)*
Symbol of Secrecy and Silence
Flower of the Virgin Mary
Good Luck Gift to a Woman
Badge of the House of York

Rose, White on Red
Badge of the House of Tudor
Flower Emblem of England

Rose, Withered
Reproach and Fleeting Beauty

Rose, Yellow
Infidelity and Jealousy
Bad Luck Gift to a Woman

Rosebud
Beauty and Youth
"Your ignorance of love is sweet!" *(Selam)*

THE WHITE CHRYSANTHEMUM.

Flowery Billet-doux, U. S., middle 19th century.

Rose-on-Soleil
White Rose within a Sunburst
Badge of the House of York

Rose of Jericho
Symbol of Resurrection

Rosemary
Constancy, Fidelity and Loyalty
Enduring Love, Devotion and Memory
"Your presence revives me!"
Herb of Aries *(Astrological)*

Rue
Morals and Mercy *(Medieval)*
Magic and Witchcraft *(Shakespearian)*
Flower Emblem of Saxony

Saffron
"Beware of excess!" *(Selam)*
Luck and Pride
Herb of the Sun *(Astrological)*

Sage
Esteem and Domestic Virtues
"I respect you deeply!" *(Selam)*
Health and Longevity
Herb of Zeus and Jupiter

St. John's-wort
Suspicion and Superstition
Devil's Flight *(Medieval)*
Charm against Evil Spirits

Sakaki, or **Shinto Tree**
Sacred Tree of Shintoism *(Japanese)*

Sakaki Branches
Farewell Gift to the Dead *(Japanese)*

Sardane, or **Herba Sardonica**
Irony, Scorn and Mockery

"I laugh at you!" *(Sardinian)*

Sedum, or **Stonecrop**
Lover's Wreath

Selam
Persian Language of Flowers

Shamrock
Flower Emblem of Ireland
Dedicated to St. Patrick

Sheaf of Wheat
Symbol of Abundance

Shooting Star
"You are my divinity!"

Snail Plant
Sluggishness and Stupidity

Snapdragon
Presumption and Desperation

Snowdrop
Hope and Consolation
"Let us wait for better days!"
Flower of January *(Occidental)*
Emblem of Early Spring
Dedicated to the Virgin Mary
Symbol of Candlemas

Solomon's Seal
Concealment and Discretion
"Our secret will be duly kept!"

Soma
Vedic Plant God of Vegetation

Southernwood
Constancy and Perseverance
Lover's Plant
Herb of Mercury *(Astrological)*

THE SNOW-DROP.

Flowery Billet-doux, U. S., middle 19th century

Speedwell, or **Veronica**
Fidelity and Sanctity
Emblem of St. Veronica

Spindle Tree
Ineffaceable Memory
"Your charm is engraved in my heart!"

Star of Bethlehem
Purity and Reconciliation

Straw, Broken
"Rupture of our union!"

Strawberry
Intoxication and Delight
"You are delicious!"
Good Luck Gift to a Woman

Strawberry Leaves
Completeness and Perfection

Sunflower
Homage and Devotion
"My eyes see only you!"
Symbol of the Sun (*Incan*)
Flower Emblem of Peru

Sweet Basil
Poverty and Hate

Sweet Pea
Departure and Adieu

Sweet William
Gallantry, Finesse and Perfection

Sycamore
Love and Fertility
Mirth and Joy

Tree of Life (*Egyptian*)

Syringa
Love and Beauty
Plant of Venus (*Astrological*)

Tansy
Easter Flower
Emblem of St. Athanasius

Tea Rose
"Our love will be fruitful!" (*Selam*)

Thistle
Defiance and Surliness
Flower Emblem of Scotland
Dedicated to St. Anthony

Thyme
Courage and Activity
Spontaneous Emotion

Thyrsus
A staff entwined with Vine and Ivy topped
by a Pine Cone
Symbol of Life and Fecundity (*Semitic*)
Emblem of Dionysus and Bacchus

Tiger Lily
Wealth and Pride

Toadstool
Symbol of Good Luck

Traveler's Joy
Rest, Safety and Playful Gaiety

Tree Peony
Love and Affection (*Chinese*)
Flower of March (*Chinese*)
Emblem of Spring (*Chinese*)

Cornucopiae, by Frederic Singleton, U. S., 1900.

Tuberose
Dangerous Pleasures
Mistress of the Night *(Malayan)*
Flower Emblem of Persia

Tulip
Symbol of the Perfect Lover *(Persian)*
"A declaration of love!" *(Selam)*
Flower of Spring *(Occidental)*
Flower Emblem of Holland
Imagination and Dreaminess
Herb of the Moon *(Astrological)*

Tulip Tree
Retirement and Rural Happiness

Valerian, or **Vandal Root**
Dissimulation and Rupture
Herb of Mercury *(Astrological)*
Fatal Gift

Venus' Looking Glass
Flattery and Pride
"You are charming but somewhat haughty!"

Verbena, or **Vervain**
Wish-granting Herb *(Persian)*
Herb of Mars *(Roman)*
Enchantment and Affection
Herb of Venus *(Astrological)*

Vine
Peace and Plenty *(Semitic)*
Emblem of the Chosen People *(Hebrew)*
Symbol of the Redeemer *(Biblical)*
Emblem of the Christian Faith *(Byzantine)*
Luck and Strength
Plant of the Sun *(Astrological)*

Vine Leaves
Mirth and Intoxication
Dedicated to Bacchus and Dionysus

Violet
Modesty and Simplicity
"I return your love!"
Flower of March *(Occidental)*
Good Luck Gift to a Woman
Herb of Jupiter *(Astrological)*
Flower of Io *(Greek)*
Emblem of the French Bonapartists

Wallflower
Friendship in Adversity
Fidelity in Misfortune
Good Luck Gift to a Woman

Walnut
Hard Fate and Trickery
Bad Luck Gift to a Man

Walnut Twins
Symbol of Good Luck *(Mediterranean)*

Water Lily
Eloquence and Persuasion
Flower of July *(Occidental)*

Wild Rose
Simplicity and Modesty
"I shall follow you everywhere!"

Wild Rue
"I like my independence!"

Wild Thyme
"You are careless and thoughtless!"

Wild Vine
Poetry and Imagination

Fruit Basket, by Frederic Singleton, U. S., 1900.

Willow
  Forsaken and Slighted Love
  Grief and Mourning (*Occidental*)
  Powers of Resurgent Spring (*Chinese*)
  Patience and Perseverance (*Japanese*)
  Flower of November (*Japanese*)
  Emblem of Meekness (*Buddhist*)

Wisteria
  Youth and Poetry (*Japanese*)
  Flower of April (*Japanese*)
  Emblem of Summer (*Japanese*)

Wreath of Flowers
  Flora's Diadem

Wreath of Fragrant Olives
  Reward for Literary Merit (*Chinese*)

Wreath of Hawthorn
  Symbol of Marriage (*Greek*)

Wreath of Myrtle
  Symbol of Marriage (*Hebrew*)

Wreath of Oak Leaves, or Civic Crown
  Award for Saving a Life in Battle (*Roman*)

Wreath of Orange Blossoms
  Symbol of Marriage and Fecundity (*Saracen*)

Wreath of Verbena
  Symbol of Marriage (*Roman*)

Wreath of Wheat
  Flower Emblem of the Ukraine (*Russian*)

Wood Anemone
  Maternal Love

Xeranthemum, or Eternal Flower
  Eternity and Immortality

Yew Tree
  Death, Grief and Sorrow
  Faith and Resurrection (*Celtic*)
  Witches Tree (*Old English*)

Yggdrasill
  Nordic World Tree

Yucca
  "Yours until death!"

Zinnia
  Thoughts about Absent Friends

Posy, from an old American Engraving, 1800.